DEAR DAUGHTER

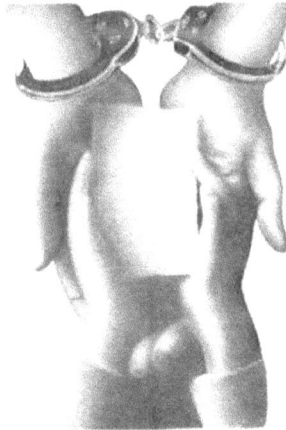

Letters of Love: A Father's Love Letter

Love, MARCUS SWAN

NATURALOSOPHY
PUBLISHING

Naturalosophy Publishing LLC
Swan@naturalosophy.com

Cover Design and Layout: Cynthia J. McCoy of CJM Creative Solutions, www.cynthiajmccoy.com

Artwork: Bolo

ISBN: 979-8-9890425-1-7

Printed in the United States of America

Dedication

My niece Saniya

May this book serve as a guide for the woman you should become. Read this book and internalize these lessons so that they carry you through life and when you have children pass them along.

My niece Emoni

There will never be anyone who loved you as much as my brother. Your dad loved all his children very much but as his only daughter, you were his pride and joy. In the times you need him the most just open this book because the love I have in my heart is the same love he had in his This is for you...

Miyale Swan

You have no control over who brings you into this world, so you are not to blame for the dysfunction around you. Let this book serve as a reminder that you don't have to be a product of who you come from; you can always choose to be better

CONTENTS

Section 1: Foundations of the Self

Section 2: Interpersonal Relationships

were unable to frame who you were as a person or where you fit into this great big world, it was my responsibility to frame this for you. It was my job to lend you my eyes to see, and my heart to understand as this would have given you a foundation from which you could build upon. And while I may be late in providing this, no one is ever a finished project, therefore it is never too late to strengthen your foundation. With this book, my hope is to provide that at the very least. And while it could never justify or make up for me not being there for you, it can at least offer you some degree of insight. Just maybe it can help you to perfect your own perspective, preventing you from having to relearn what I had to learn through trial and error. By offering you the lessons derived from my experiences, I am not trying to dictate to you, my love; instead, I am trying to save you from the same pain, misery, and valuable time many others have wasted. For this is your birthright from me, to be provided with a trustworthy perspective you can lean on to start your journey. And this is something fathers are best suited to provide, as there is no one who would know better of what awaits you on your journey.

Because of my imperfections, I ask

for your understanding. As I am reminded every day of how I have failed you as a father, I am in dire need of your compassion. Whenever you consider how I have failed you, I ask you to consider that my father also failed me, and that his father also failed him, so on and so forth. But this failure of us fathers is not due to a lack of love, but rather a lack of understanding. It was necessary that your father first learned the lessons he needed for his journey, because only then could he provide you with the lessons you need for yours. But the irony of it all is that life does not always provide us with the luxury to complete such a task. Circumstances and time do not always provide us the leeway to learn both for our children and for ourselves simultaneously. So often, our time is cut short before we are capable of adequately fulfilling such a task. Life did not provide me with the luxury of being there for you as result of me being subject to my own life lessons; however, it did allow me the opportunity to gather these jewels so that if I ever had the opportunity, I could share them with you. While the jewels I offer may come belatedly, they are nevertheless still valuable. And even if these jewels do not reach you in time to facilitate your journey in life, they could facilitate the journey of your children or anyone else whose journey is just beginning. So, I ask you to read with an open heart because through this book, I offer you fatherly guidance. I know that this is not how you imagined receiving it, but I can assure you as unorthodox as it may seem, the guidance you find in this book will rival that of even the most perfect father. I say this not in arrogance but in sincerity of my intentions. My only hope is that you consider these jewels with an open mind, but most importantly an open heart.

Love Marcus Swan

INTRODUCTION

Dear Daughter,

A daughter without a father is like a planet without a Sun. A planet that drifts through the cold, blackness of space, all alone, having nothing to influence her orbit and no gravity to keep her grounded. She sadly swans through space divested of light, warmth, and life. As your father, I was supposed to be your sun; I should have been there to provide you the warmth, light, and direction you needed. I know at this point it is irrelevant to tell you how I did everything in my power to get back to you. But I'll tell you anyway, I tried everything in my power to get back to you. But much like the universe, the laws of gravity confined me to my orbit away from you and everything else I loved. But there was not a day that I didn't wonder about what you were doing, how you were feeling, and what you were thinking. I imagined you watching everyone else enjoy the security of a father, and how it must have felt not having yours. Not having anyone come to your basketball games, not having me to brag to about your grades, and not having me around to show you how important you are.

But even despite my absence, in spite of me neglecting to provide you with my warmth, light and direction, here you are emanating with more warmth, light and direction than I could have ever provided you. Rather than becoming some lifeless planet, you somehow became a powerful star that sustains everything around you. How is this possible? A planet that evolved into a blazing star! This speaks directly to how special and miraculous you are. It speaks to how much God loves you. You may wonder why and how I could speak of God, and my reason is because you are my proof of His existence. You may feel as if you have suffered from my absence, but I was the one who suffered from yours. I cannot convey how difficult it is living with the fact that I deprived myself of the pleasure, honor, and blessing of being there to watch you evolve in real time. Again, it was not you, but I who was deprived. I will go to my grave resenting that fate would not have me be there to teach, nurture, and protect you. I envy your mother for the love, respect, and honor she has earned from you because of her enduring presence in your life. I envy her for the investment she has made, and her ability to now sit back and reap the fruits of that investment by seeing the beautiful young woman you blossom into with each passing day. I often think to myself how I must be cursed to have planted this prolific seed and yet be prevented from cultivating it to harvest. I offer these words to you as my love letter, a father's love letter to his daughter, to reassure you of how loved and cherished you will always be to your father. There is nothing that can deprive a daughter of a father's love. My love for you knows no depth; it is deeper than all the oceans in this world. A depth which cannot be penetrated or explored.

There are many fathers who have never received love and therefore do not understand how to give it. But I can assure you, this was not the case with your father. I came from love, so I know exactly what it is. So, when I tell you I love you, it's not just empty echoes. By the time I leave this earth, it may not be said that I was the perfect father, but it will be understood that I was someone who loved his daughter.

I honestly believe that you can best recognize a man's love for his daughter through the love he has for his mother. Thus, the love I have for you is a direct reflection of the love I have for the woman that brought me into this world. And the first thing you must understand about my mother is that she is my hero. The majority of *the people you encounter in life will have allowed their hearts to grow bitter and cold because of the terrible things they've been through. Such people eventually grow incapable of loving anyone or anything. But while anyone can use life's tragedies as a justification to be cold-hearted, it takes a truly resilient individual to still maintain the ability to love. This is my mother. Despite everything, she has never allowed it to deprive her of a loving heart. To this day, I have yet to meet anyone with such resilience. I admired her even as a child and though I was much too young to put into words why I loved her so much, I now realize it was her spirit. I loved her refusal to be put in a box. I loved how she refused to allow anyone to define who she was and who she wanted to be. She was the very first flower I witnessed to emerge from the concrete. Not only do I love her, I respect her. All this love I have for my mother is what enables me to love you. This is why I love how graceful and unfazed you are by your circumstances. This is why I love you for your refusal to let anyone put you in a box. This is why I love you for wanting more than what life is offering you. This is why I love the potential I see in you, but most importantly, this is why I love who God made you to be. My hope is that you never, ever doubt my love because everything about you was made for me to love.*

Love Dad

SECTION 1:

FOUNDATIONS OF THE SELF

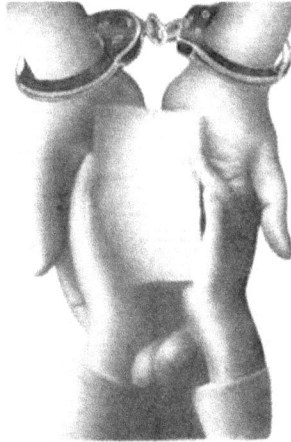

1

Jewel of Strength

Dear Daughter,

May this letter reach you in strength, fortitude, and empowerment. So, you may understand that weakness serves as the biggest threat to your survival, my love. If you consider history, it seems the greatest advancements in power have come about through the greatest advancements of human exploitation. This demonstrates the correlating relationship between power and weakness; it demonstrates that there can be no power without weakness and there would be no weakness without power. This truth tells us that only the strong will survive in this world.

And this is a motto we must live by because if not, it may very well be the reason we cease to exist.

As a young woman, your being strong entails you are embracing an unapologetic mentality for not being weak or passive. As those who are strong must understand the necessity for strength. My love, being strong is your audacity to believe even when everything around you convinces you to do otherwise. Being strong is divesting yourself of all weak qualities, worthless mentalities, and ignorant mind- states. Being strong is a conscious choice you make every single day that you wake up in the morning. It is the choice to fight the good fight, to not give up or call it quits. It is a choice not to allow your flaws and mistakes to dictate how you view yourself. Being strong is making a choice not to let the vicissitudes of life overwhelm you. Being strong is not seeking sympathy or pity from those who will use such moments to empower themselves over you. Being strong is a commitment to exercise your God given free-will no matter what the scenario. Being strong is your exercising your ability to choose. Being strong is to endure what you go through but conduct yourself as if it is inconsequential. Being strong is never surrendering under any circumstance but fighting until the very end, fighting until your very last breath. This is the essence of being strong and this is something you must become to not only survive but thrive in this world. Being strong is the example you must establish for those who will follow you. Because for people like us, we don't have the luxury of being weak. Throughout history, we have barely survived when putting forth our strongest efforts, so what chance could we ever stand in weakness?

My daughter, be strong just as

your father is strong. Be strong just as your uncles are strong. Be strong just as your mother is strong. Be strong as your grandmothers and all the women who came before you were strong. Do not become the individual who finds pleasure in lamenting your weakness. Carry on for no other reason but life will carry you along either way, as life has yet to stop and wait for anyone. This is not to say that you will not experience moments of weakness but only that you must not ever succumb to such moments. Every time you fall you must get up on your own and dust yourself off.

If you ever lose your way and misplace your strength, remember that it will always be found in your ability to let go. Those who are strong are never overwhelmed by weakness because they understand how to let go for moments at a time when it all becomes too much to bear. Letting go can be found in the brief moments of life when all our troubles and worries dissipate. Moments when we temporarily get lost in something as trivial as a movie we watch or a song we hear; moments when nothing is weighing our hearts down. You must embrace these moments and do not condemn yourself for having them.

These moments serve to ground you about the experience of life itself. Essentially, these moments teach us how temporary life is and that there will come a time when nothing matters as much as it seems to now. During these moments, you are given the ability to recalibrate and continue the fight. This is where your strength will always lie. It is in these moments of letting go that God is providing you a restoration of strength so you can then approach your circumstances with power. Remember that being strong does not mean you will always be the strongest. Being strong is not always winning the battle. But being strong is an uncompromising willingness to fight and struggle no matter the situation. To be strong is to reject the idea that you are weak. So always be strong my love.

Love Dad

2

Jewel of Valuing Yourself

Dear Daughter

May this letter reach you in a state of peace and positivity but most of all may it find you validated and self-assured of your immense worth. May you always be self- assured of your worth in all the various roles you will take on in life whether it be that of daughter, sister, wife, mother, or friend. So much of knowing your worth is in understanding that your true purpose is to fulfill each of these roles with the upmost commitment. Thus, your true value lies in how honorable you are to your mother and father, how loyal you are to your siblings, how devoted you are to your husband and children, how compassionate you are to your grandparents and grandchildren, and how dependable you are to your friends. This is what dictates our worth in this life. Do not fall into the trap of thinking your worth is in how many followers you have on social media; or in how many men lust to be with you, or in the texture or length of your hair. It is not in the brightness or darkness of your skin, the shape of your figure, nor in your job title or credit score. Your value will always be found within your inner circle because only those to whom you bestow your true value can assess your true worth. If you were to spend your whole life giving the best parts of yourself to a world that cares nothing about you, you would then have to accept whatever value the world gives to you no matter how uncaring that assessment may be. But if your life is spent giving the best parts of yourself to those in your world, it is they who will continuously assure you of your value and who will appreciate and treasure you to the utmost. This is where you will find your value.

My daughter, I say to you that you are a woman of integrity. A woman of the highest value. Your worth is so immense there is no scale that can quantify it. Your every thought is of the upmost importance, your words resonate deeply, and what you feel is of great concern. In a world where we question if Black lives really matter, I assure you beyond any doubt, you matter. And you will always matter to me regardless of any matter that can ever matter. So let this be the only matter you never call into question. But it's not enough to know you're worth, you must also internalize your worth. My love, you must believe in your self-worth whole-heartedly. It is imperative you embody this idea of your self-worth and never allow it to be taken from you. As there is no greater tragedy than the woman that allows herself to be stripped of the idea of her own self-worth. Such women often end up as statistics having ransomed their humanity to someone, they falsely believe can internalize their worth for them. God knows, my love if only it were possible to internalize this idea for you I would do it 100 times over; your mother would do it 100 times over. But this idea of your worth is something only you can internalize into reality. So do not presume anyone can do it for you. For it cannot be done. The most handsome boy on the planet cannot internalize your worth for you, money cannot internalize your self-worth, and status cannot internalize your worth. It is only you that can do this. And by internalizing your worth, you will have transformed yourself from a shy girl into a lion- hearted woman. Believing in this very idea will serve as the ritual to adulthood. Contrary to what you were taught, it is not when you have your first period or lose your virginity or have your first child that makes you into a woman. True womanhood is triggered by the realization of your true worth and never have it taken from you. But internalizing your true worth is not just about putting the highest price on yourself, it is more so about coming into a realization of how priceless you are. Knowing your value is the realization that you are one of one. As there is no one in the world that can provide to the world what you provide in the exact way you provide it. There is no one that could replicate the same type of energy you give to the world through your smile and laughter. There is no one with your warmth and compassion. There is no one able to express their love so passionately. Who else is there with your swagger and finesse? If no one has told you, you are certainly one of the coolest girls to walk this earth! Your loyalty defies gravity. Your beauty encompasses space and time. Your faithfulness shines brighter than any star in the sky. And this is what makes you a one of one. But the relevant question is do you believe it? Do you believe you are one of one? I pray you do because it is absolutely the truth. If you were not to believe this, you would destabilize the world. Because there are many people around you that are relying on the belief you have that enables their belief. And how could you ever help someone believe in their worth if you don't believe in yours. This is how you are one of one, because you how much you are needed. Your father needs you. Your mother needs you. Your siblings need you, your children will need you, your nieces and nephews will need you; the world needs you.

None of this is to imply that your value is solely predicated on the people that need you, but only to point out the obvious and unavoidable truth, which is how one-sided any relationship with you can be. See in business, anytime there is an inequity in a two- party partnership, the party with the least leverage will seek to increase the value they bring to the partnership. One of the leading causes of successful partnerships falling apart is a discrepancy between which partner is bringing more value to the business. I use this analogy so you can understand your father's absence in your life. The reason I was not there when you needed me was not due to my lack of love for you, and it was certainly not because you're not important to me, but actually the complete opposite. Your father's absence was a result of his own desperate attempt to increase his value in your life. My absence was a product of my own sense of inadequacy, my own selfish interest. There was a time when I believed that a father's value lay in what he contributed financially to his children but over the years I realized this is not at all the case. Now I know a father's value is not measured in materialism but in humanism. Humanism is a father's ability to promote the well-being of his children. I want you to understand your father is deeply flawed, but not at all flawed by nature. My own hands have brought about my flaws, which in no way extends to you. The outcome of my life was a product of the ideas I chose to believe. Though you are my daughter, those foolish ideas I internalized have no bearing on the type of human being you will become. You are the sole architect of who you will become through what you choose to believe. My hope is that you understand you are not defined by the choices of anyone but your own. You don't have to embrace the flaws of your parents, but you can exploit our strengths to your benefit. It is a principle that a man's daughter can only receive the best parts of her father. So, you must not question your value as a result of my choices.

I do not understand how life can make the most important

people in society feel as if they are the least important and the least important people feel as if they are the most important. The world is so full of people propagating their personal brands as if that could supplant their self-worth. But true value and self-worth cannot be measured through materialism. Your value encompasses money because your integrity can never brought. The innate drive of yours to seek Truth and Justice for yourself and the people you love is priceless. Your refusal to be cheated out of your God given rights finds perfection through your fighting spirit. Your mere presence provides a resoluteness to the world; neck swinging, teeth smacking, eye rolling in all. You are the voice of reason in any circle you occupy. You are the balancing factor which society cannot do without. I pray you never lose sight of this lesson.

Love Dad

3

Jewel of Exploiting Trauma

Daughter

May this letter find you in only the best of states, those conducive to love, integrity and healing. My soul aches as I think about how I wasn't there to shield you from the troubles, disappointments, and heartbreaks of womanhood. It is all too common for young girls to have experienced trauma in a multitude of ways that cannot be explained; trauma that many girls choose to endure silently; trauma that varies in intensity and degree. Many women whose behavior we consider unstable, and erratic can very will be trauma they are attempting to bury. As your father, I just want you to know that I understand. In dealing with your trauma, I want you to know you can always talk to me about anything. You don't have to bury your pain because you feel like nobody else cares about it, because that is not the case. There will always be someone you can reach out to about what you are dealing with, even if it is not me.

However, I understand that there are certain wounds I cannot heal, no matter how hard I try. . I understand, that there are some things better left unspoken. But just know, you don't carry them alone. I want you to know I will always share in all your burdens. People often assume sharing and expressing trauma is the best thing to do but sometimes, refusing to give unnecessary life to something is the best way to let it die. We must always confront the source of our trauma, but afterwards, we should not feed it in a way that brings us further agony. Trauma is the single thing woman growing up without fathers commonly experience. But it's also the same quality that renders such women stronger than the rest. Your trauma provides you with your resilience. Do not be afraid to let the trauma you experience in life serve as your driving force. As it can serve as your motivation propelling you to your destination. My daughter, learn to extract the power and energy your trauma provides you. Let your trauma be gasoline that feeds your fire. But you must always control this fire and use it for your purpose rather than allowing it to burn you.

The things we go through in life do not have to define us; we have the power to utilize anything as emotional gasoline. Those of us who are destined to blaze the most important trails will always have an adequate amount of trauma as fuel for the journey. But the only way possible you can blaze this trail, is by making the conscious choice not to succumb to the wounds you sustain throughout your journey. Yes, there will be many scars and they will be painful, but eventually the pain will subside, and these scars will heal. But you must not preoccupy yourself with the pain itself but rather focus squarely on the destination.

Though it may not seem like it in the moment, the pain and trauma you experience at an early age can be your saving grace. While something may hurt in the moment, that pain is oftentimes preserving the best parts of you. While young, you will meet many people who are not overburdened with trauma, who have not experienced the adversity you have in life. But as God as my witness, these individuals will eventually become victims of their lack of pain and struggle, and as a result will exhaust much of their potential early in life. While you on the other hand, will use the pain you experience as guardrails to lead to your gradual and steady growth. Thus, you should never run from your pain but rather embrace it; exploit it in a way that is conducive to your maturation. Few realize just how indispensable pain is to the development of character.

The pain and trauma that life gives in life is not a curse or an indication of God's lack of love or indifference towards you; but rather a meaningful provision necessary for the accomplishment of your God given task. When you realize that trauma is a means to your advantage only then will pain relinquish its negative impact on you. Thus, your trauma is not to be stored, hoarded, or preserved for showcase or contest, it is to be used, exercised, and employed for progress. You must become the definer of your journey. Never allow society to masquerade your pain in mockery, because this is not a sign of their compassion. Embracing a victim mentality is usually a debilitating mechanism. Don't allow yourself to be relegated into a victim by people with no genuine interest in your advancement. Society has made this term victim synonymous with casualties, prey, and dupes. Society has conditioned us to view victims as people who have been involuntarily deprived of something. But the reality is that whatever situation that brought about your trauma has not deprived you of anything or at least anything you can't recover. Trauma does not take but rather gives. This label of a victim invites weakness. Therefore, you must always remember, she who overcomes her trauma is anything but weak. The women who surmount their adversity and exploit their trauma for power are TAKERS. These are the true alphas of society as such women prove themselves unbreakable. And there is no one more intimidating than the woman who cannot be broken. Thus, if someone ever tries to classify you as a victim as a result of some circumstance you have overcome, tell them you are not a victim as this word is synonymous with weakness, but instead tell them you are a taker. Because you took an imperfect situation and used it for your perfection.

Not only can our trauma serve as our motivating fuel, it also provides us a rare opportunity for reconstructing our deeper self. It provides an opportunity to perfect ourselves. Neurology has taught us how trauma can be a means of enabling our nervous system to reach a state of neuroplasticity. During this state of neuroplasticity, we are more capable of creating newer and stronger neurological brain networks relative to self-transformation and learning. What this means is you will never be more capable of self-improvement than in times of pain and misfortune. Therefore, you must use any instance of trauma as an opportunity to rewrite the hard drive of your heart in a way conducive to your success and power. There are countless people in a state of dissatisfaction, yet they are psychologically ill equipped to change their condition. These types lack the necessary trauma needed for self-evolution. On some intrinsic level, we all understand the value of trauma and the power it provides by our tendency to overdramatize even the slightest offenses we experience. Ask yourself, who in America is not a self- alleged victim of some traumatizing experience? Everyone claims to have gone through something, but only those who have truly experienced trauma will demonstrate its significance after having conquered it and become takers. Therefore, embrace the struggles you have overcome as an emblem of honor. Wear it with integrity, dignity, and grace.

Love Dad

4

Jewel of Spirituality

Dear Daughter

I pray this letter finds you in a state of spirituality and unshakable faith. A state of true faith. And not the type of faith characteristic of praying to the sky for something to fall out of the clouds; nor hoping and wishing all your problems away; nor waiting for some savior to come and rescue you. While this may provide others a sense of security, let your faith be rooted in your willingness to tread uncharted territories in your search for true spirituality and faith.

While here on this earth, we human beings are inherently afflicted with a constant sense of displacement.

We cannot escape this deep-seated voidness. It is a voidness of loneliness we cannot overthrow and an incompleteness we cannot make whole. Theoretically, the underlying impetus behind everything we doo may be our unconscious drive to fill this unfulfillable void. For example, the woman who grows up without a father, who then marries a possessive husband oftentimes, is looking to fill the void of a caring father. But no matter how father-like her husband is, this void remains unfulfilled. And the reason so is that a missing father was never the source of the actual void to begin with. This woman does not understand her void is not a product of something in the physical but a result of something deeper, something spiritual. She does not realize nothing she does will ever do away with this void. Changing one's identity or sexual orientation will not extinguish this void. Falling in love cannot extinguish this void. Friendships cannot extinguish this void. Pleasures cannot extinguish void. Success cannot extinguish void. There are people who even denounce religion and become atheists as a means of ridding themselves of this void. Addicts use drugs and alcohol to try to numb this void. People immerse themselves in entertainment and distractions to disregard this void.

And after doing all of this, the void remains all the more still intact. After exhausting every imaginable means of doing away with this void, many even opt to commit suicide as the last fatal alternative. Thus, every insecurity, every uncertainty of who you are or where you belong, every longing and desire are all just products of this underlying void that you, I, and every other human being cannot escape. This void will permeate every faucet of your life and cannot be satisfied through anything physical. Very few realize that this void can only be placated by means of a spiritual phenomenon; the idea of a God that is everything and all things.

I understand how difficult it may be to acknowledge the existence of a higher power when you look at the state of society and you see no reality of God. I understand how godless the world may seem, but it is not for the human being to define the reality of God. Instead, our purpose and emotional stability will only become clear through the Reality we recognize as God. There are physical aspects of the human self that can be sustained through physical means but then there are spiritual aspects of the human self, such as this void, which can only be sustained through metaphysical means. Therefore, it is a metaphysical belief in God that will provide you relief from this metaphysical sense of incompleteness you experience. Thus, the more devoted you are to your respective religion, the more complete you will find your sense of self and your sense of purpose in life. But you should not approach the idea of God as if it can be found in any one time or place. It is too great a task for our limited intellect to grasp. Instead, you must seek God through the prism of your immediate reality. It is only by recognizing God as Reality that your relationship with God will be provided substance. In life, you will inevitably encounter a plethora of false realities.

Your journey of spirituality will begin the second you try to do away with these false realities that cloud your perspective. The more studious your search for Reality, the more intimately you will have interacted with God. And in corresponding fashion, the more divested you are of this materialistic society and its falsehoods, the more invested you will be in true Reality. This means that, true love and devotion to God lies in ones detachment from the deception surrounding you, only then will you truly seek and thirst for Reality. Only through this particular state, is one afforded an opportunity to experience True Reality.

My intention is not to force upon you my religion but only to clarify exactly what it means to have a relationship with God. As there are many individuals claiming to have a relationship with God, oblivious to what such a relationship entails. There are three ideas active in all the major religions of the world, which are, God is Truth, God is Love, and God is Peace. If one were to sum up these ideas, we would have to conclude that a real relationship with God could only entail an actual search for God. Thus, a true relationship with God is a search for Truth, Love, and Peace. If God is truth, then a pursuit of Truth is the basis of this relationship. And the pursuit of Truth entails a search for what is not temporary, what is not illusory, and what is not substantively false. Consider that, if God is Truth, how could a relationship with God ever be based on any book that has fallen victim to misrepresentation? If God is truth, should not the scripture of God also be pure of human deception. With that being said, Truth cannot be relegated to just some scientific verification; as Truth itself is a spiritual phenomenon impossible to verify. Truth is transcendent by virtue of its nature to be both simultaneously natural and supernatural, tangible, and intangible, provable yet unprovable, and static but yet astatic. Even as transcendent as Truth is; it is so meek in nature that it is intimately recognizable to everyone and all. Thus, your relationship with God begins with your search for Truth.

If God is Love, then your Love for God will reflect your love for Truth. And to love the Truth is not a feeling, an emotion, or a sensation. A Love of Truth is your willingness to defend the Truth, it is your willingness to embody the Truth, but most importantly, it is your willingness to make Truth the underlying anchor of your Life. Never mistake the love of God to be merely praising, screaming, and shouting. Nor should you mistake the love of God to be a blind conviction in an idea one refuses to intellectually scrutinize. Nor is the love of God the empty praise people sang after receiving something they desire. These are all instances of those who love their own personal idea of God more so than the true Reality of God. You will realize your Love of God when you develop a Love of Truth. You will realize your Love of God when you personally love what God Loves and hate what God Hates. And the only way that one could ever know such a thing is through Truth.

And if God is Peace, then you're search and love for Truth will eventually lead you to an overwhelming sense of Peace that soothes this void I mentioned earlier. This Peace will also bring you into unity with your life purpose. But more than anything else, the Peace you have with your Truth will be a direct reflection of your relationship with God. Many individuals claim to have Peace with their truth, but the measure of true Peace lies in the absence of anxiety in the face of another's love of truth. On your journey, you will find many people uneasy by anyone devoted to a religion different from theirs. These individuals obsessively aspire to propagate their truth, not as a product of their Love for it, but a means of monolithic assimilation. Because of their deep insecurity, many people are driven to ensure that their truth becomes everyone else's truth, even if it's by coercion. But this is not Peace. Such an individual has not found peace with their truth.

The totality of Truth, Love, and Peace are composites of True Reality. Thus, a relationship with God is an engagement to Reality. A commitment to Reality. A marriage to Reality. There are people who spend their entire lives striving to escape Reality, preoccupying themselves with illusions and false realities. But the true lovers of God are those devoted to remaining steadfast in it, no matter how tempting the alternative. God is physically inaccessible by nature and can only be sought through spirit and intellect. With that in mind, one must consider that without religion what other means would there be to achieve such an goal. God has made religion the spiritual directions to Reality. But just as it is the case that not all religions will lead you to God, not all religions will lead you to Reality. One of the most important decisions you will make is what religion to embrace. My deepest hope and desire is that your choice leads you to Reality.

Love Dad

5

Jewel of True Beauty

Dear Daughter,

If I were to try express to you how beautiful you are in just words, I could fill up the Atlantic, Pacific, Antarctic, and the Indian oceans, and it would still not be sufficient. As God as my witness, your beauty lives, breaths and speaks. It needs no defending, validating, or campaigning. It cannot be disregarded or understated. Nor can it be denied or relegated. Your beauty will fight, struggle, and overpower anything trying to diminish it as it resists being intimidated. Your beauty refuses to accept inferiority. For this reason, it is imperative that you wear your beauty unabashedly because it is the crown through which God ennobles you. The very beauty emanating from your lovely skin is reflected in the history of Queen of Sheba, Cleopatra, and Nefertiti of Egypt. People often hate what they have to acknowledge, and your beauty demands its respect and reverence from any and all. Your nobility shines ever so brightly, challenged by neither the luminance of the sun nor the radiance of the moon. My daughter you emanate pure majesticness, compelling everyone in your immediate presence to honor it by merely seeing you.

There are various manifestations of beauty, but the beauty you possess is the embodiment of the most original order of royalty. There are few things in life more beautiful than a king or a queen in their full glory. It is understood that Kings, Queens, and those of royalty beautify themselves with majesty rather than delicacy. Thus, your beauty is not meant to prettify your disposition but instead to dignify your existence. Do not allow yourself to yearn after what society parades as beauty, but rather embrace your beauty as an embodiment of your royal nature.

Look at yourself in the mirror and recognize the Queen God has made you to be because this is where your true beauty lies my love.

God has distinguished your beauty, so why would you ever seek to render it undistinguishable? Daughter, your every feature is unique, defining, and cosmopolitan. God has made you from all the best parts of the humanity. From your ancient Asiatic eyes, your regal Egyptian nose, you're rich Caribbean Lips, your foreign Middle Eastern eyelashes your glorious European cheek bones, and your sacred Amerindic eyebrows. Oh, and I cannot forget your best quality by far, your Nubian skin complexion. But beauty itself is so diverse and multifaceted it cannot be approached as if it were a hierarchy. Instead, we must approach beauty as the spectrum it is. Therefore, the true measure of beauty will always lie at the very center of this spectrum. As the center would illustrate a perfect balance of all forms of beauty. Never worry yourself if it seems your beauty does not overlap with this Western ideal of beauty.

The true extent of your beauty could never be measured, it is unquantifiable because it is infinite. But like all things in life, even beauty works by laws of nature. Thus, God has decreed that your beauty must flourish in coordinated stages just as it is the case with all things in nature. For example, flowers are beautiful not merely because of their appearance, but because of the amazing process, they undergo in route to reaching their ultimate form. We look in awe at the beautiful red rose fundamentally aware of its humble beginnings. We understand that it began as just a seed in the dirt, but after slow and gradual nourishment, it eventually evolved into something unexpected. In large part, this is what makes the rose so beautiful, its evolution in reaching its potential and I pray you understand that you are no different. Similar to the red rose, the ultimate perfection of your beauty is manifesting itself more and more with each day. Be patient my love, allow yourself the opportunity to grow and maturate to prime form. Do not rush the perfection of your beauty because like the flower, the butterfly, and the trees; you are likewise in a continuous state of evolution. Let your natural beauty develop at its natural pace and only then will it reach its true potential. There is a beauty in everything in life; but every form of beauty has its own process of evolution. Daughter, as beautiful as you are the brilliance of your evolution is even more stunning to behold. Therefore, every morning, I want you to look in the mirror and say, 'While today it is true, so beautiful I awake, tomorrow will certainly be more so the case!'

Love Dad

6

Jewel of Protecting Your Womanhood

Dear Daughter,

I honestly believe that there is a divine wisdom behind the roles we are pre-assigned in life. If it is in fact true that life is not the product of random accidents, then there would have to be a reason life would allocate which roles we are to carry out. But it seems more than ever people are questioning these roles as well as whether there is an underlying reason at all.

Yes, everyone has a right to orientate himself or herself as they so choose; but there still remains an underlying question of why fate assigns us our respective roles in the first place. If we are ever to reconcile this question, we must first grasp the nature of what the term gender actually means. Aside from it being just a reproductive distinction, the true meaning of the term gender is essentially a particular function each of us contributes to creation. If it is true that God is All Knowing and does not make mistakes, the predetermination of any particular function can only be one we are most suited to carry out. Natural selection is thought to be the process that assigns each individual its role in the order of life. But if this theory is in fact true, it must also be the byproduct of the wisdom of God. Thus, we should not dismiss the idea that our natural function may provide us the best opportunity to make our greatest impact on the world.

Let us consider this from a spiritual perspective, when God created woman; it was not merely to serve as a reproductive companion for man's carnal disposal. With the creation of man, life itself was suddenly provided reality; but it was not until the creation of the woman that life was provided its purpose. Prior to the existence of the woman, life had no purpose. It had no direction. It had neither a past nor a future. Theoretically, you my love are the symbolic representation of purpose, and you provide it to everything you engage. I want you to always remember that your essence is not solely reliant upon any man. Even though, man and woman are co-dependents. As a woman, you have a purpose and independence aside from the male species. Therefore, it is impossible that any man could ever validate or invalidate your essence. And dare I say it is also impossible for you to invalidate your own essence as a woman.

And as somebody who knows and loves you, I can say with due *certainty that you will always experience this urge to make any and everything around you meaningful and of purpose. This is why you are so passionate; this is why you care so deeply. Daughter, this is why you wear your heart on your sleeve about things that seem trivial to everyone else. It is a byproduct of your nature to provide purpose to the world. This very function God assigned to you is not perfected in superficialities but rather in how <u>willingly</u> you embrace what you were destined to provide. This is the true essence of your womanhood*

Society conditions us to believe we must all carry out our assigned functions in a particular type of way. This shows itself most clearly in the exaggerated ideas of masculinity we have in our culture. For example, many males are self-conscious about telling their wives, girlfriends, sons, and daughters how much they love them due to the idea that expressing one's feelings is unbecoming of a man. My Love let me be the first to tell you, your father has never embraced this idea. Fully secure in my manhood, I could go on and on and on expressing how much I love you. Nonetheless, such preconceived ideas of masculinity and femininity do exist in our culture. Thus, you must beware of allowing society to question or cause you to doubt your purpose. Even if you do not exercise your natural function the way others deems it appropriate, this does not make you any less worthy of fulfilling your purpose. Just because you feel more comfortable in a pair of Jordans rather than a pair of hills does not make you any less a lady. Again, I am not dictating which particular function you should embrace; I'm just reminding you that regardless of the choice you make, you are nonetheless fully equipped to carry out the assigned function life has selected for you.

The essence of your womanhood is not predicated on whether you identify with Barbie dolls and the color pink, or how comfortable you are dressing in a way that exposes your physical qualities for the world to see. This is not what makes you a woman. The real tragedy in our culture is that, if the average girl is not preoccupied with such things, we encourage them to question their womanhood as if there is only one way to exercise femininity. But in the same breath, we champion woman empowerment. My daughter, may you never allow your womanhood to be put in a box by anyone. May you never allow society to dictate upon you what you should like or dislike; what you should identify with or not. May you never allow society to impress upon you what you should be preoccupied with as a woman. May you never allow the culture to rush you into sexuality as we so often do with young women. May you evolve into your womanhood at your own pace and in your own space. And when any woman tries to concern you with what she thinks about your femininity, tell her, "How I exercise my womanhood is my prerogative!" My daughter, protect your essence in a time when the essence of womanhood is under attack. This is true empowerment.

Love Dad

7

Jewel of Intellect

Dear Daughter,

I pray this letter finds you in perfect wisdom, knowledge, and understanding, as I cannot emphasize to you enough the significance of the intellect God has put in your heart. You and I come from a culture that undervalues intelligence and enlightenment and shuns anything outside of its limited grasp. Which is why concepts such as logic and reason have been made inconsequential to your beautiful eyes. The world knows that if someone such as my daughter were to empower her intellect, it would change everything; it would interrupt the entire balance of power. Perhaps, this is why society conditions you to believe that as a woman you are to prioritize emotion over logic. They try to condition you to believe that the greatest fulfillment you will ever find as a woman is the validation you receive from men. However, this is a lie because there is no greater fulfillment in the world than intellectual fulfilment. Society seems to dissuade you from seeking enlightenment as if you yourself are also not an idea of God. As if God did not also give you two eyes to see, two ears to hear and a heart to understand. Or did he limit your understanding in any respect? Of course not, because to do so would prevent you from recognizing his transcendence. And never will you truly appreciate the majesty of your Creator until you comprehend the majesty of His creation, something which can only be accomplished through your intellect.

As your father, I can admit, I did not appreciate the true value of the intellect for far too long. For generations, I casted off my rationality in exchange for materiality. Rather than aspiring to intellectualism as a means to my evolution, I opted to become a materialist, which ultimately resulted in my devolution. For so long, I could not educate you because I was not educated. I could not enlighten you because materialism had jaded my enlightenment. Only after understanding the true impact of intellect, did I realize that I must help my daughter to do the same. Therefore, I come to you, just in the nick of time. Just as you are growing into this beautiful, strong,

and determined young woman, urging you to awaken of your intellect.

In your search for Wisdom,

knowledge and understanding do not just look, but seek to realize. Do not just hear but seek to apprehend and do not just process phenomena, but also seek to grasp it. Don't strive to be this specialized expert the education system conditions others to be, but instead strive to be an intellectual. For the expert strives merely to memorize and relay information with no deeper insight. While the intellectual strives to grasp and penetrate into the essence of ideas providing one with a wholistic grasp of everything. The key to awakening your inner genius begins by first approaching life and everything in it for what it truly is, an idea. The meaning of the term intellect is the capacity to interact and navigate the various forms of ideas in a way that enables you to evolve. Therefore, by empowering your intellect you will have the ability to conceive and illuminate the most powerful ideas in the most naturalistic way. And the more adept you become at this, the greater your genius will be.

Many people see no value in intellectual enlightenment thereby failing to cultivate their genius to power. Sweetheart, you must not become one of these people. At all costs, you must diligently seek out your genius. The adversity that life has so harshly cast upon our ancestors has contributed to jading our genius. It is because of this that we should not leave this earth before having reawakened our God given intellect. To do otherwise, would be a disservice to both God and our descendants. It was through a long and arduous struggle that our intellect was suppressed, so it will be through a long and arduous struggle that it will be reawakened. But if you commit to seeking it, you will find it.

Every single day you get up to go to school, don't approach your education as a burden or something you do only to obtain a grade from the teachers. No, approach your education as a means to your personal perfection. Approach knowledge as a weapon you can use at your discretion, because life is a fight, and you will need it to win the fight. Approach your education as your destiny because self-enlightenment is your life mission. Therefore, no matter where life takes you, do not shy away from this mission because its accomplishment is everything.

God was once said in a scripture that, "My people suffer for a lack of knowledge." So, the very thing that threatens everything you want out of life will be what you lack in knowledge, or your lack of knowing. The reason the majority of people in this world are poor is not because of any type of disability or inability but rather an ignorance of some sort. It is due to the lack of understanding about some valuable form, function, or formula they need to apply to their circumstances. The reason America is one of the most affluent countries in the world is due to the advancement we have in the various fields of knowledge. In a sense, it is not really those who have and have-not but rather those who know and know not. Creating the life you deserve comes down to you either knowing how to acquire something, who to acquire it from or where to acquire it. My daughter, I would imagine that your plan is to be a success in everything you do, right? Thus, your approach to everything must be one of knowing before that of doing. Because there can be no doing without first knowing.

Therefore, in everything you do seek knowledge thereof. If your plan is to play basketball, first seek out the knowledge it will require to be a great basketball player. If your plan is to have children, first, seek out the knowledge it will require to be a great mother. Before you start a business, you must first seek out the knowledge it will require to become a successful business owner. Before you take someone into your intimacy, you should first seek out the true substance of that individual to determine if they are worthy of your presence. Because in the end, if it shall happen that you fail in anything, it will be due to what you did not know or what you did not understand.

Love Dad

8

Jewel of Cultural Independence

Dear Daughter,

While young, our view of the world is always optimistic, as the world appears beautiful and full of promise. But the older you get, the more you'll realize that this world is not as beautiful and full promise as you once thought. One day, something heartbreaking will happen and it will make you realize how evil and corrupt this world really is but it's important that you not allow it to overwhelm you. Don't let it corrupt your nature. Because to do so would leave you hopeless and hope is one of the indispensable tools you will need in life. I speak from experience when I tell you there will be days when you have nothing or no one to lean on but hope.

When you are considering the immoral state of society, don't do so in totality, but rather break things down as you would fractions. And after doing so what you will realize is that culture serves as the determining factor for much of the madness we see today. For every evil and atrocious act carried out in the world, history has always provided an evil and atrocious individual or group of individuals through which to attribute such acts. Perhaps this is history's way of concealing the fact that these evil and atrocious individuals are ALWAYS products of evil and atrocious cultures. Cultures, which are responsible for providing these individuals the evil and atrocious ideas they come to embrace. And it is often the case that these ideas will always seem evil and atrocious to those outside of these cultures, but for those within them, such ideas are not considered such but instead are considered the complete opposite.

While in school, you were taught about the history of America in regard to American colonization, Slavery, and Jim Crow Racism, which culminated in the death and oppression of millions of Native and African Americans. However, these acts have never been attributed the same atrociousness as other acts in history because there is no one individual such acts can be attributed to. Therefore, when teachers speak about the history of America, they will try to minimize these atrocities. In a roundabout way, this shows the evil and atrocious culture that existed back then and to a large extent the present day. This shows that evil acts are essentially secondary to the evil culture from which such acts derive.

Without our realizing it, our cultures mold us and dictate the type of human beings we ultimately become. Therefore, if you don't want to be a product of your culture, you must have the objectivity to be critical of your culture. Critical, meaning, you must not presuppose everything in your culture to be right, honorable, and worth following. Nor should you be indifferent to the things going on around you. You must be objective enough to understand the complacency and limitations of the culture you come from. I say all this to say, please my love, do not become a product of this culture we come from, but instead be a product of your own intellect. Be a product of everything you know to be right. In most cases, when we embrace the culture, we will always become something lesser than who we were meant to be. Everyone sees their culture as a reflection of themselves. We have centered much of our lives on culture; it has now become our collective sense of pride. Which is crazy when you consider how commercialized culture has become. Companies marketing their products now understand that in order to sell a product to a particular segment of the population, they must first infuse their product into the culture of that segment. As a result, you will now see many commercials attempting to depict what they believe our culture to be about. And the worst part about it is we who make up the culture, can no longer distinguish the difference. So now, like everything else in society, our culture is no longer a product of who we are; it is now a reflection of what society thinks we are.

And it is for this reason that you must never be afraid to intellectually disassociate yourself from your culture. In doing so, you become a leader to yourself as well as to those oblivious to what the culture is imposing upon them. I have yet to figure out why we are so attached to culture but for whatever reason it is like the sun to our galaxy. Without realizing it, many of us are so head over heels in love with culture we willingly subject ourselves to humiliation and degradation from it. But not only do we have this deep love for culture, but there is also a desire to be loved by the culture. I know this to be the case because there was a time when my sole preoccupation was to be loved by the culture. There was a time when the only guidance I was receptive to was from the culture. There was a time when my only purpose in life was to be acknowledged by the culture. But as I evolved, I began to see that the world and life in general was bigger than my little culture. When I became an adult, I began to regard myself more important than the culture itself thus allowing me to see how insignificant my culture truly was.

Daughter, if you ever want to see how attached we are as a society to the validation of culture;

just watch any type of award show. Watching these award shows will not only show you the nature of a particular culture, but also how invested people are in their particular culture. We act almost as if, when we die, we will stand before our culture to be judged rather than before God. In conclusion, do not idolize your culture. Do not let it limit your potential. Do not be afraid to pursue something different than the culture you come from. Do not chase after your culture and do not condemn yourself if you should lose touch with it. Because at that point, the question is not why you do not identify with the culture, but rather what is it about the culture that has swayed someone such as yourself from it.

Love Dad

Section 2

Interpersonal Relationships

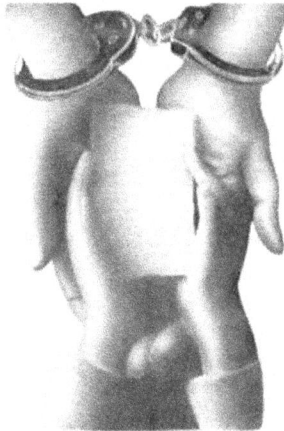

9

Jewel of Managing Emotions

Dear Daughter,

As the compassionate and empathic young woman, you are, I know you are keenly sensitive to anything others are attributing to you. We sometimes stifle our own growth by relegating ourselves to the opinions of others. By over concerning ourselves with other people's opinions, we willingly allow those people to put us in the box they think we belong. My daughter, you must quickly reach the realization that people will never regard you the same way you regard yourself and sometimes this even includes family. Most people give themselves so little consideration it would be crazy to think they could ever give you the consideration you deserve.

What I am telling you is that you must not be overly sensitive to the things people say or think about you. Do not give unnecessary weight to any and everybody's opinions, because such opinions do not matter. Besides, the majority of people you encounter will be delusional and will have opinions not grounded in any type of reality or truth. I want you to think about how flimsy your character would be if you just relied on random opinions of others to shape who you are. You would be very much like everyone else in society, an intellectual and emotional wreck. You would be someone with no firm grasp of anything, someone high one moment and low the next. And to be this way renders you nothing at all.

While we are developing ourselves early in life, we should not rely solely on our own opinions about ourselves because our opinions can easily be skewed and subjective. We must keep a very select group of people we know are objective, people we know will tell us the truth; the opinions of these individuals are the only ones we should take seriously. Outside of these select few, we must not be overly invested in what we hear from anyone else. Strive to provide yourself with a psychological curtain from all of the useless opinions and ideas others will try to impress upon you. This curtain will ensure that any idea people attribute to you whether in the form of a joke or a clinical assessment, will bounce off you and have no effect whatsoever. But to acquire such a disposition is a gradual process. It requires letting the things you hear about yourself fall by the wayside rather than allowing them to affect you emotionally. When you remain steadfast in this practice over time, eventually it becomes second nature. In essence, this requires that you become a less emotional person altogether. While we can never do away with emotions and feelings all together, we do have the power to limit how emotions and feelings dictate our conduct. In most cases, our emotions will always be attached to some idea we have unduly embraced. Therefore, when you are gripped with emotion, analyze the idea empowering the emotion and by analyzing the idea you will exercise greater control over both the emotion and your conduct. The key to controlling your emotions is in knowing exactly what is triggering them.

Love Dad

10

Jewel of Male Insight

Dear Daughter,

I pray this letter reaches you in a state of peace, humility, and most importantly understanding. As there are so many things we have all yet to understand about life. But as a woman, nothing will be more elusive to your understanding than that of the male species. There will be times when you think you have grasped what men are all about, and then something will happen to cause you to question everything you thought you knew. There will be women in your life who will try to convince you they have us figured out. Nevertheless, as a man, there is no one more qualified to provide you a glimpse into the nature of men then the one that brought you into this world.

The first thing you must understand about the male species is that we are dependents by nature. We men are emotionally dependent upon a particular quality that only you, the female species, can provide. Now, before you jump to conclusions, that quality is not what you think. The quality I am referring to is nurturance. More than anything, we men depend on the nurturing quality characteristic of the female species. The vulnerability to female nurturance is deeper than just an emotional disorder; this is more a spiritual predisposition. Let us say that in the beginning of time when God created man, God is quoted to have said, 'it is not good for man to be alone,' thus bringing into existence the female species. Therefore, while God did not create the female solely for purposes of nurturing man, she was created in such a way that she accomplishes such through her very nature. But the female species is not just a nurturer of man; God made woman the nurturer of Life.

The male begins as an

innocent little boy, oblivious to his place in the human hierarchy. Therefore, in the beginning, his overbearing selfishness seems natural and even charming to the woman responsible for taking care of him. As a child, his vulnerability makes him rather easy to love. But in time, he evolves to realize his place then transforming from the helpless child into the self-- indulgent young adult. And from a self-indulgent young adult, into a brutish man. Almost as if overnight, his physical appearance changes, he grows taller and stronger in stature. He begins developing facial hair, and his voice suddenly becomes deeper. All of sudden, he no longer resembles the little vulnerable boy he once was, as his physical and spiritual nature bears itself more and more to the extent that nurturing him becomes less natural and more of an emotional burden. The woman looks at him and no longer sees the helpless, endearing child, but begins to see the self-seeking and rapacious man. A man outwardly preoccupied with indulging his own selfish desires. She begins to see a species looking only to control and dominate.

But what many women fail to

realize is that even in spite of his manly exterior, deep within him lies that same vulnerable child, that same boy in need of nurturance. Contrary to what many may think, men are not just seeking the affections of women solely for sexual amusement. The basis underlying man's ardent desire for women stems largely from the emotional refuge she symbolizes to him. There is no clear cut definition that can wholly outline this quality of a woman's nurturance, as it is the byproduct of her nature. Her delicate and sensuous stature, her sweet and soft tone of speaking, her womanly mannerisms, even the way she expresses her ideas and emotions;

all resonate profoundly with the male species in a way that provides a peculiar type of validation needed for his own existence.

In the beginning, before God tended to man's lonely plight, man had likely roamed the garden questioning his place within it. This traumatizing experience had to have rendered him both physically and emotionally displaced. Before the creation of the female, man must have contemplated his lonely existence in this gigantic realm and felt a sense of irreconcilableness. Thus, it was only when he encountered his female counterpart that he could then reconcile his place in the world.

Therefore, the woman can be said to have abridged man's perception of space and time, thus becoming his physical and emotional refuge in the process. In essence, this is the true condition of the male species.

But the condition of man fluctuates as his perception of his surroundings change. Thus, the men of yesterday are not the men of today. Or in other words, the condition in which you remember men to have been in the past will not reflect the same condition you see them today, tomorrow or in the future. Which is to say that history, time, and circumstances have always contributed to the substantial makeup of man. The male species is helplessly susceptible to his elements, which explains why the state of the male species is always in flux. This being the biggest reason man is at odds with his intended purpose. With each passing generation, man falls more and more out-of-sync with his true nature. His heart's preoccupation with materialism has caused him to lose sight of his innate potential. It has brought about a disconnection from his true self. He no longer knows who he is, where he comes from, or where he is going. It is for this reason that man cannot ascertain what he wants until he subsequently realizes what he needs. This imperceptiveness is oftentimes why he aspires so devotedly from one thing to the next, aloofly disregarding that thing after losing sight of its immediate significance. But it is not only the significance of a thing he loses sight of, it is essentially his own purpose. This cycle causes him to continuously organize and reorganize the dynamics of his relationships. And it is for this very reason that one day he seems to take interest, the next day, not so much; One day he seems considerate, the next negligent. One second a perfect gentleman, the next, a bestial degenerate. Whenever you see such erratic behavior from the male species, understand this is nothing more but a conflict of purpose taking place within him in real time.

Many of the men/boys you have met in life are on the losing end of this battle of purpose. A battle that has relegated their existence and depleted their understanding to such an extent that many of them now serve no spiritual, intellectual, or physical value to you, the world, or even themselves. These individuals will provide you the worse impression of the male species. But I bid you not to base your general perspective of men on these particular individuals, as they will render you hopeless.

Whenever you encounter these types of men, beware. Guard your modesty and respect because such men seek only to gratify themselves at anyone's expense. Remember, just because men were created greater in stature does not make them invincible. What you lack in stature as a woman, you make up for in emotional and intellectual understanding. Man's primary weakness will always be his ego. Therefore, by nullifying his pride you nullify his power. And because of how much we depend on the validation of women, there is no one more capable of bruising man's pride and ego than you. Most men do not operate from the heart and are thus oblivious to inner workings of the self, so God has made you strong where man is weak. But this is also not to imply that you should be an emotional tyrant either, my love. This is to show you your means of protection as a woman.

Most men opt not to embark upon the spiritual journey of life and therefore do not evolve. As most of the men you meet will be immature and not on your level. You will have become a woman well before most boys will have become men. But again, not all men will be the same. There are bad men but there are also good men. Therefore, even if it doesn't appear to be the case right now, there will be someone with potential, someone worthy of your nurturing. You will know such an individual because without realizing it, you'll find yourself naturally tending to his vulnerabilities; reminding him that the internal battle he struggles with is nothing more but his refusal to accept what he cannot change; his purpose. But you will not remind him of this by directly saying it but simply by just being you. It will be through *your conversation, your kindness, your attitude, your charisma that you will convey such. It is your natural capacity to nurture along with his natural vulnerability that serves as the most basic link bonding the male and female as one. But when this time comes, <u>preferably</u> <u>after college,</u> you must be very selective with whom you provide nurturance. As it is unbecoming of a dignified women to lavish it upon just anyone. It is not your responsibility to nurture just any man. For example, in the religion of Islam women are encouraged not to speak too softly but rather with a firm tone of* *voice when interacting with men outside of their families and who are not their husbands. Many people may see this as controlling, when in reality; this is only to protect the woman's honor. When you understand the true essence of the woman, you understand that she is by nature a source of nurturance for men. And when you understand the true nature of man, you will understand that he will overbearingly seek to self-indulge nurturance from any and every woman he can. Thus, the female must conduct herself in a certain way to avoid being unduly exploited of her nurturing. As you mature, it is important that you learn how to interact with men without necessarily nurturing them. Only reserving such nurturing for the man, you have so graciously chosen to provide it to.*

Love Dad

11

Jewel of Recognizing

Superiority Complexes

Dear Daughter,

I would love nothing more than to have brought you into a world of peace, happiness, and harmony. I would love nothing more but for your life to have been stress-free from beginning to end. I would love nothing more but for your heart to have remained free of any type of pain, heartbreak, fear, or worry. Unfortunately, this is the unrealistic thinking of a father. Even if I had been the perfect father, I still would not have been able to protect you from such vicissitudes. In fact, my deep love and unrealistic desire to protect you would have only did the opposite. There is nothing I could have done that would change the fact that there is a force at work in this world aimed at devaluing your worth as a human being. This antagonistic force was created many years ago for nothing more but to label and categorize you in a way that renders you obsolete in comparison to others. And this force is so powerful it has operated for generations with impunity not only through people but through laws, institutions, and social customs.

Throughout history, many

people from all races and backgrounds created movements to challenge this force, and even manage to weaken the power through which it functions. Rather idealistically, society has now begun to celebrate the various blows to the force's power, now indoctrinating the masses to believe that this force is no longer a threat and essentially nonexistent. In fact, society is so convinced of this; it has set out to make the very mention of this force taboo to the point that in the future any notion of its existence will be attributed to superstition or exaggeration. But contrary to what many will have you believe; this force is very much in existence and very much still a threat. In theory, this force is similar to a living organism, in that, like other living organisms on the verge of extinction, it has now evolved into something much more sophisticated, something better suited to adapt to its changing environment. Thus, this force is now operating much more insidiously in its objective to relegate your humanity than it has in the past. And one of its more subtle means of accomplishing this is through

conditioning   you   with   an
inferiority complex.

*Unbeknown to many, one of
the   dividing   factors   between
people in our country, aside from
anything   else,   is   domestic
confidence. Domestic confidence
is perhaps the most fundamental
form of confidence as it provides
the structure for any framework
to   be   had   in   terms   of   further
development.   Domestic
confidence is a particular type of
confidence   that   can   only   be
fostered   in   one's   sanctuary
habitat. This   sanctuary   habitat
can   encompass   one's   domestic
family,   domestic   neighborhood*

but most importantly one's domestic country. Unfortunately, this country limits who it affords this type of confidence to. Those precluded from such confidence have to navigate their way to success without it. Thus, people who look like you will often excel in spite of having to deal with feeling uncomfortable, unwelcome, and unworthy in their own skins throughout the journey. This lack of confidence is one of the primary reasons our children fail to realize their potential. This lack of confidence is why we do not see ourselves as being beautiful and are constantly seeking validation from others. This lack of confidence is why so many people that look like you have become complacent and stagnant and do not see themselves as being leaders. My love, when you see those that look like you who become shells of themselves when around their racial counterparts. Or those who do not feel comfortable in their own skin around people who do not look like them, understand that these people lack this type of confidence as a result of an inferiority complex.

This inferiority complex is a product of a force that seeks to *deprive certain individuals of this domestic confidence. The immense power of this force is demonstrated by the numerous **ways** in which it is able to instill in people this inferiority complex. Because there is no resource it cannot exploit, it has utilized people, laws, institutions, and economics to accomplish its objective. And we are often implanted with this mentality without our ever realizing it. For example, if it were to happen that a little girl went to school and had some little boy who did not look like her, call her ugly, and she did not yet have a strong enough identity to reject* *this idea, it could very well initiate the beginning of an inferiority complex. If it were the case, that certain laws were put into effect that afforded one group of people certain advantages it did not afford to other groups, as it where with the Jim Crow laws in the 1980'2, this could very well initiate the beginning of an inferiority complex. If there were institutions in our country designed to protect and serve everyone yet these institutions prioritized only one group of people above everyone else, such being the case with many of the police departments in this country it could very well bring about an inferiority complex. And if the top one percent of people overseeing the economies of the world had*

a common understanding that they must strive to always monopolize the wealth from anyone that didn't look like them, this would surely bring about an inferiority complex. This force at work is so powerful it even exploits the people who looks like you to do its bidding. If

you haven't experienced this already, it will certainly be the case you will experience arrogance and contempt from the very people who look like you simply because their skin tone is lighter than yours or darker than yours. Or because they come from a different geographical region, or because they grew up under different financial circumstances from you. And this as well can bring about an inferior complex.

The biggest mistake you can make in life is allowing yourself to fall victim to any type of inferiority complex. There is a difference between being humble versus accepting some idea that you were made inferior to another human being. Yes, you should absolutely have humility, as there is not a more beautifying quality for a woman. But you should never accept the notion that you are inferior to anyone. By embracing an inferior mentality, you are willfully relegating your humanity to something lower than God created you to be. And why? Why should you be something lower than God intended you to be. That is like the lion trying to be a gazelle. Or the shark trying to be a dolphin. We should never aspire to be something lesser than what our nature calls us to be.

In life, there will be people who try to treat you as if they are innately superior to you, and you must defiantly reject this idea. There will be laws that seem to hold you back, but you must overcome such by being someone who knows and demands your rights. There will be institutions that try to render you unworthy and underserving, but you must disregard this idea by realizing and walking in your true potential, regardless of their lack of validation. Because as your father, you do not have my permission to accept any idea that you were made inferior to anyone other than God. And while I forbid you from embracing an inferiority complex, this does not mean that you should develop a superiority complex instead. As this is the same mentality of those who desire to exalt themselves over you. Do not go from one extreme to the other but instead seek an equilibrium. Be humble enough to understand that your life will come to an end like everyone else's but be confident enough to know that when it happens, you will have left your impact on everyone around you.

Love Dad

12

Jewel of Individuality

Dear Daughter,

How are you? I hope and pray this letter reaches you in the best of spirits. Never allowing life to deceive you about who you are as a person. As I think back to when I was young, it took me a while to come into my own as an individual because for much of my young life, I was always around my friends. Like most teenagers, my friends and I were glued to the hip. We hung out all day every day. But by being immersed in my circle of friends, I compromised and hindered the growth of my own individuality. In retrospect, now I see that my reality as an individual was my sociality.

During that time, if someone were to ask me who I was as a person, I would have defined myself in terms of my neighborhood or my social group. I have a theory that the tendency we have to take on a social identity rather than our own self-identity is rooted in a subconscious idea currently operating in society that the only way to exist to the rest of the world is by presenting ourselves through the prism of our social group.

As it stands, this is what seems to be occurring as most teenagers are consumed with their social life. They spend the majority of their time with friends, and when they are not with them, they communicating via cell phone or social media. And this goes on for years and years, and in some instances continues into adulthood. Now a days there is never a lapse in time when one exists as an exclusive individual to oneself rather than to one's social group. In most cases, there is no opportunity during adolescence to free oneself of this social influence. The ultimate effect of being overly preoccupied with the reality of one's social life is that you begin to develop both a social self and an individual self. Which is essentially a fragmented identity. This can be the root cause of serious mental health problems. In such instances, you will become one person when you are around your friends or particular group of people while becoming a whole other person around everyone else. I know it may seem crazy in light of how much you love your friends right now but consider that throughout life, friends actually will come and go. A social identity predicated around a particular friendship will become psychologically problematic when that friendship ceases to exist. At that point, then who are you? What good is everything you invested in that social identity when it comes time to move on to a new social setting? Will you then create a new social identity? This is exactly how we lose ourselves.

One of the things I can assure you is that things will change regardless of what we have planned. Life is a journey, and one of the saddest realizations of life is that not everyone is headed to the same destination or moving in the same direction or moving at the same pace. I assure you; you will not end your journey with everyone you started it with; eventually, there are friendships you will leave behind and those that will leave you behind. There are friendships you will outgrow or that might outgrow you. There are friendships that have to be sacrificed for the sake of progress. God places particular people in our lives at certain times and for certain reasons. You do yourself a disservice by overinvesting in friendships to the extent that you deny yourself new ones. It may be that a future friendship will benefit you more than an existing one. When your identity is fragmented, you will sacrifice all of the fruits of life just to preserve a social identity; that is not even actually your true self. And the irony is no matter how much you try, you will never be the social identity you create for yourself, as you cannot escape your self-identity.

None of this is to imply that you should entirely deprive yourself of the fruits of friendship but only to convey that friendships are just that, fruits. They are sources of fulfillment one should enjoy on occasions. But in no way should any friendship be the focal point of your life because at that point your friendship exists as your single life purpose rather than having your friendship exist to guide you to your purpose. At this moment ask yourself; do you utilize friendships for your fulfillment or for your identity? Do people tell you that your social life is toxic? Have you allowed yourself to be overly invested in the validation of your friends? Have you ever passed on something solely because of what your friends may think? If you were to lose your current friendships, would it deprive you of your identity as an individual, or would losing a friendship make life any less meaningful to you? The answer to such questions reveals whether you are compromising your self-identity and whether you are hindering your individuality.

I hope that you are always able to preserve your individuality or rather, preserve your individual sense of self. My hope is that you disown this idea that your identity as an individual can only be a product of your social network. My hope is that you can mold your identity into something independent of your friendships. And that you retain your independence of self by taking time to befriend yourself. My hope is that you explore your potential and not hold yourself back because of some social   attachment   you   do   not want to let go.

Love Dad

13

Jewel of False Saviors

Dear Daughter,

My daughter may this letter reach you in peace and in good spirits. I believe that one of the most difficult lessons in life for people like us is realizing that we cannot save everyone or rather anyone no matter how much we love them or desire to do so. And when I say save, what I mean is become the intervening cause that redirects their path or reshapes their identity. When you love someone, there's this natural tendency to want to be the very cause of their salvation. When you love someone, you typically see them in a light far brighter than they even see themselves. This being a product of our compassion will often lead to our delusion because our contriving of someone's potential does not mean it actually exists. The tendency we have to see people in the most favorable light stems from the idea that there is goodness in everything and everyone when unfortunately, this is not the case. We so desperately want to believe that our children, parents, friends and loved ones are good people even when they continue to prove this not to be the case. Our unwillingness to accept this reality causes us to try in prove otherwise. Therefore, it happens that in our attempt to save them, we only delay the inevitable. There was a show I used to watch called

Intervention. The show was about family and friends who would try to create these group interventions as a means to save their children from the consequences of drug addiction. And it was fascinating to watch this show week after week because it demonstrated how hopeless it was to help people that didn't want to help themselves. It demonstrated that the only intervention capable of saving someone was divine intervention.

The odd thing about those of us who believe we can save those we love is that we often become prey of the very people we try to save. Those we try to save are in most cases well aware of their condition and do not change simply because they desire not to change. In reality, it is almost arrogant to think we can convince someone that they need to be saved from themselves. People do not become who they are by coincidence; people make themselves into who they are conscientiously. Any notion that someone needs saving suggests they don't have a right to exist as they wish to be but rather as you wish them to be. This is like telling someone their defective and need to be fixed, but only you can fix them. This is very insulting, but this is exactly what we do as we over invest ourselves in another's salvation. Which is why in most cases, this same individual will recognize the hopeless need others have to save them, providing them a perfect opportunity to exploit that need in the process. For this reason, you must never have more of a desire to help someone than they have to help themselves.

And nothing serves to help someone more than the actual experience itself and the situation they go through as a result of their actions. So, the best way to help someone is by letting them go through their trials and tribulations rather than intervening to try to save them. Not only should we not be so quick to render ourselves somebody's savior, but we must also not embrace this idea that we ourselves need a savior. In our culture, there is a debilitating idea that we should be patient and rest our hopes in the surety that something or someone is coming to save us, when this is not at all the case. There have been people who have died waiting on a savior that never came. There have been people who have wasted the majority of their lives waiting for a savior to come in to make everything better, whether this savior was in the form of a brother, a mother, a father, a husband, or a wife. You must understand that regardless of how bad things get in life, nothing, or no one is guaranteed to save you. The only salvation you are guaranteed is the salvation you provide yourself. Therefore, the moment you become your own savior is the moment you find your saving grace. We live in a time where there are no heroes; therefore, we must become heroes to ourselves. And by doing this, it may just happen that you help others understand what they must do to save themselves.

Love Dad

14

Jewel of Real Love

Dear Daughter

As always, I pray this letter reaches you in a state of peace, humility, and most of all love. May you experience love in your home and love in your travels, love in your friendships, love in your partnerships, and love in all of your enterprises and endeavors. May love come to permeate your entire existence. In life, we often learn and approach the idea of love based on what we are taught, never seeking its true essence. As a woman in this culture, I can only imagine how you were taught to approach this idea of love. Many women are taught to equate how much someone loves them by how much someone is willing to give and sacrifice for them. So, if you were to believe someone would give their life for you or give you all their money, it would demonstrate that they love you most of all. But while sacrifice can in fact be an expression of one's love, too many of us consider this the only expression. When you see sacrifice as the only means to love you become self-centered and arrogant in your expectations because sacrifice is a unilateral concept, while love itself is a bilateral concept. In most cases, sacrifice is nonreciprocal while love is reciprocal by nature. Yeah, you could sacrifice your life to show someone you truly love them, but the bigger question is will that person make the same sacrifice for you. If not, this act of love has now become life's greatest tragedy. My daughter, love is not just me dying for you; but also, me doing whatever it takes to live for you.

Love is not addition by subtraction. Love transcends quantitative value. Throughout life, you will hear numerous people claim to love you, but you must assess the authenticity of this claim by how much interest they have in your wellbeing. And when I say, wellbeing, what I mean is their consideration of your natural self. Those who truly care about your wellbeing desires to see you reach the state God has intended for you. There will be many people willing to make investments in the interest of your worst self, but this is not at all love. For example, if you had a desire to be a drug dealer, and someone where to help you reach this desire, this would not be a testament of their love for you because doing so would be detrimental to your natural wellbeing. Aside from being invested in your wellbeing, love is also loving you apart from the purpose you may serve for them.

As you will realize, many people care only about the purpose you serve more than anything else and this is not love. For example, let's say someone begins to love you because you're the person that makes them laugh, but I promise you, the second you stop making them laugh, that love will vanish. You will recognize genuine love by the passion one has to bring about the perfection of your wellbeing. Love is not a warm feeling one has or does not have; it is a pledge of loyalty you make to someone or something. Love is a loyalty to cherish one's wellbeing regardless of the circumstances.

The cold reality is that not everyone in this world loves you. Thus, you should not overextend yourself by loving just anyone. To love someone and to show love are two very different things. I can show someone an act of love, but this does not necessarily mean I love them. I can give my enemy a drink of water just before he dies as an act of mercy, but this would not at all mean I love him. As I said earlier, love is a pledge; and a pledge can only be valid when entered into by all parties involved. To love someone who does not love you in return would defy one of God's most basic laws of life, self-preservation.

Don't lose yourself in the trappings of love. If you shall ever find someone able to reciprocate the love you can give, approach it primarily as a means of alliance rather than reliance. Approach love to solidify your stability. But in doing so, make sure to be modest and do not go out of your way to parade your love. In fact, always be aware of such people who excessively speak of how much they love you, because in some cases it could be a smoke screen. I once grew up with a girl who had a habit of declaring how much she loved me, but later in life, that same girl ultimately revealed herself as an enemy. Love is something innately deep, so when it is present it does not need to be acknowledged, it is simply understood. This is not to imply that you should never express love to your loved ones, or that you shouldn't tell the people you care about how much you care. I just want you to understand that people will use even something as pure as love to disarm and take advantage of you. So don't let it happen.

I have seen many people confuse love with the desire to be loved. Daughter do not allow yourself to be consumed with this romanticized idea of love. There are women who desperately chase after love in relationships, never realizing that they are actually chasing a super-charged idea of love. In most cases, these women do not actually love their partners but instead only love the idea of being in love! They continuously feed this idea as they listen to love songs, watch romantic movies, and read love stories all to reify this feeling of being in love. As a result, there is not a more sought- after illusion in society than falling in love. This experience many people perceive as falling in love is nothing more than infatuating oneself. It is the belief in the idea of love, which captivates so many people. But this phenomenon of infatuation does not last. It is only a temporary sensation.

Thus, anyone claiming to have fallen into love will invariably fall out of love just the same. The marriage statistics over the past 50 years will substantiate this. None of this is to imply that you should not become infatuated with anything, because this is impossible. There will certainly be people, places, and things that will naturally arouse your infatuation, but you must not allow this temporary feeling to become an idea you believe in and internalize. Whenever you encounter something that infatuates you, rather than approaching it like some transcendent experience that will last forever, approach it well aware that it will dissipate as suddenly as it arose. In fact, you should be assertive in seeking out anything that will help diminish your infatuation as a means of promptly doing away with this feeling, because infatuation is not based in reality. Infatuation is not a natural element of human experience, and we know this because it is impossible for anyone to remain in this state continuously. Nor is this state conducive to our survival. Had the first human beings that walked the earth been infatuated with anything other than their survival, we would most likely not be here today. My point is that you do not have to fall into infatuation with someone to love them. In fact, most of the things we become infatuated with are unhealthy for us. Do not be deceived by this idea of love.

Love Dad

15

Jewel of Sibling Relationships

Dear Daughter,

My daughter, who I love so very much. I feel it necessary to prepare you for one of life's greatest mysteries. The mystery of biological siblings. There will be no journey more mysterious than the one you share with a sibling as you transition through life. There will be no one who knows you more than these individuals. The dynamic of any relationship we have in life is a mere reflection of the relationships we have with our siblings. There are so many days that I wish I could go back in time and be a better big brother to my siblings. I often wish that I had spent more time with them, taught them more about life and expressed to them the importance of loyalty and sticking together no matter what happens. Daughter, take advantage of this time when you and your siblings are still young and be the best big sister you can be. Don't just be a big sister that scolds them when they do something wrong, but a friend to your siblings. Create as many memories as you can with them. Don't just rely on them to assume how much you love them, show it, and tell them. As there will come a time when they will no longer see you as the big sister they cherish and respect but only someone with whom they are competition   to prove   their independence.

One of the great mysteries in life is how the very same siblings you come into this world with may ultimately become people you do not recognize by the time you leave this world. Regardless of how much you love your siblings, do not to be surprised if you were to realize that they do not share that same love in return. You will grow up loving your siblings and will likely convince yourself that by virtue of your familial ties, loyalty will always exist within these relationships. But the cold reality is that this is not the case. As important as loyalty is in this world, it is not guaranteed from even your siblings, which is one of the most heartbreaking things you will ever realize. Regardless of how much you look like your sibling, or that you share the same biological DNA as them, they will all become their own person. Which means that you just never know what type of person they will grow up to become. Yeah, they may be one particular way as kids, but this has nothing to do with who they will become as adults. People will create narratives to justify their actions, but the reality is that life will always expose who we truly are. It will expose our deepest feelings whether it is jealousy, hatred, or just plain indifferent. Thus, your deep love for your siblings will not be able to change who and what they may become. In fact, this concept goes well beyond siblings and extends to all of your family. The older you get, the more you will realize that the idea of family is not what it seems. Daughter, I hate to tell you this but do not allow yourself to believe those you call family will automatically care about your wellbeing. There may be members of your own family who envy you, despise you, and regard your existence to be no different from any other random stranger. Thus, there will be family members that try to steal from you. There will be family members that gossip about you behind your back. There will even be family members that try to devalue your self-- worth. Keep in mind; it is always those closest to us that do us the most harm. As it stands, the term family means nothing more but the people with whom you share a common ancestral lineage. So, with this logic, all human beings are family because all human beings descend from a common linage. Therefore, in other words, your family does not have to be limited to just those you share a biological connection with, your true family are those with whom you share a common loyalty, a common idea, or a common way of believing. Thus, your family can be anyone. If any of your biological family were to show themselves detrimental to your wellbeing, you must sever these ties rather than holding fast as if such bonds are unbreakable. In scripture, God demonstrates that family ties are not absolute when he told Noah that his own biological son was not in fact his true family. Even Jesus once said when alluding to his biological family, "who are my family but those who do the will of God". God demonstrates through both instances that it may be the case that we have to redefine whom we classify as family. Make no mistake; this is not me telling you to disown any of your family. To the family who show themselves true in their love and loyalty to your well-being, you must return this same love and loyalty. But you should not over invest yourself in a family that does not over invest themselves in you. You must see yourself as an individual apart from your family. Let it never be the case that you deprive yourself of what you could be because it does not conform to what your family has in mind for you. For example, don't be afraid to go to college because you worry about leaving your family behind. Let it never be the case that you live to serve your family's purpose rather than your own.

Daughter do not blindly be your sisters or brother's keeper if those same individuals are not your keeper. And most importantly, do not allow your family to expect something from you they don't also expect from themselves. There will be those that expect you to be your reliable, stand-up self when it comes to family, but who will allow and accept others to be less than such. We often see the world as we think it should be rather than what it truly is. But the reality is that the very first murder to have ever been committed in this world was Cain killing his brother Abel. Which means the very first act of treachery came from a family member. So essentially, what I am telling you is to love your family, be there for your family, stand up for them, and offer them your upmost loyalty even if it means dying for them. But if anyone in your family were to ever show themselves unloving or abandon you when you need them or fail to stand up for you or show themselves disloyal, then they just may be showing you that they are not your family at all. In such instances, rather than entertaining a facade, you would do better to cut ties with such people and focus on your true family.

Love Dad

16

Jewel of the Truth & Deception

Dear Daughter,

May this letter reach you in a state of Truth. For we live in a world that tries to discredit, distort, and essentially eliminate Truth in all of its various forms. For that reason, I assure you, deception will surely try to permeate your life by way of people, places, and situations. In other words, I bid you to prepare and brace yourself, as you will soon realize the true depth of deception operating in this world. The older you get, the more it will seem as if life's ultimate purpose was to deceive you all along. Deception and illusion is so engrossed in our reality that the three major religions of the world all allude to a judgment day when all deception and illusion will be made clear, and the truth will be made apparent to everyone. This demonstrates that as we get closer to the end of time, deception will be so prevalent it will become almost impossible to distinguish truth from falsehood.

For this reason, it is important that you find someone wise and well advanced in age and share their company. Speak to them and allow yourself to see through the lens of their souls. I promise you, what you will come to feel above any and everything else is their disillusionment with life. The look of disarray you see in their faces will be one of disappointment after having realized the many deceptions of life. It is in their seniority that the true illusion of life becomes most evident. The meaning of being young is one's pursuit of life with the belief of what it should be, while the meaning of growing old is the acceptance of life after having seen what it truly is.

For this reason, do not just presume anything to be true. Always leave room to consider that something may actually be just another illusion. As there is nothing more hurtful than having realized, you have been deceived by something you presumed to be the truth. To ensure that you never end up on the wrong side of truth, you must make yourself an over-analyzer. This is not to say that you should over-analyze every detail of every matter of life but that you should over-analyze everything disguised as <u>truth</u> to ensure it is not a deception. Every person you meet you must patiently vet out what deceptions lie in their hearts; expose the different faces they put on and take off. You must approach every situation looking for the deception that lies under the surface. Because by doing this you ensure you never become a victim of another's deception. Because the worst type of victim you can be in life is a victim of deception. Therefore, I bid you to *make it one of your life's goals to die having not been deceived by anything. May you leave this earth after having exposed everything for what it is. Even if this is an impossible task, let it still be the essence of who you are because it will make you a truth- seeker. Beware of deception. Keep in mind that it engulfs you with every turn and at every step. Understand, that no matter how decent of a person you are, how much good you do, or where you go, no one is immune from deception or being deceived: this is the one fight no one can turn the other cheek to or walk away from; deception is the one enemy you cannot make peace with. It is your sole responsibility to struggle to prevent yourself from being deceived because by neglecting to do so you could contribute to your own downfall.*

Love Dad

17

Jewel of Overcoming the Street Mentality

Dear Daughter

How are you, my love? Today, I am writing this letter in awe of how intelligent and strong- minded you are, allowing me to envision just how promising your future could be. But in the same breath, it also leads me to distress over all the things which stand to threaten this promising future. I am of the belief that in every culture, there are certain ideas that blinds one's perception so that we only see the world through the prism of that idea. For us, there is one particular idea we have absolutely been blinded by an idea so prevailing it is almost impossible to avoid. This idea is the phenomenon we call, 'the streets'. Daughter, this idea of the streets is so entrenched within the culture we come from it has encompassed everything from music, movies, books, and clothing. As of today, it is the very essence of our culture. But the sad reality is that nothing has claimed more lives of people that look like us, or left more people hopeless, ignorant, and complacent than this idea of the streets. Without minimizing my accountability, I can acknowledge now that the streets is one of the reasons I am writing you this letter in passing rather than having taught you such things in real time. The streets is why many of us fathers have become statistics to either mass incarceration, gun violence, drug addiction or just defeated by life's circumstances to the point that we are useless. This idea of the streets has stagnated and essentially demoralized generations upon generations of not just fathers but our people in general. The reason you do not see an abundance of intellectuals, scientists, and doctors that look like you is because the streets have claimed the potential of such people before it could ever be nurtured and realized. The streets have taken some of the best people and transformed them into some of the worst people you could imagine. The streets is now one of the primary sources of misery for all those confined within its psychological parameters.

But what is so odd is that the same individuals who are continuously victimized by this idea, will nonetheless still honor and cherish the idea of the streets. Myself included, I now struggle to overthrow this idea from my heart. The streets have been the downfall of everyone around me yet so many of us are still captivated by this idea. There are countless men in prison who have been permanently deprived of their freedom because of the street-life they once led, yet these same individuals will spend most of their time in prison still infatuated with the streets. Such individuals will constantly reminisce about the streets, listen to street music, read urban novels, binge on movies and TV shows depicting street life and also strive to stay in the know about what's going on in 'the streets'. Also, you will often see grieving mothers and fathers who have lost children to the streets, but these same mothers and fathers will often be those who themselves took pride in being products of the streets which in some cases contributed to their child's demise. Whenever a parent directly or indirectly expresses any type of belonging or allegiance to the streets, the child will unconsciously seek their sense of belonging in it likewise. Thus, you have the cycle of incarceration, drug addiction, crime, and teenage pregnancy.

Even if it is the case that we are in many respects products of the streets, we must not relegate our reality solely to the streets. Which means that we must not limit ourselves by embracing the streets to be our only reality. You will hear this mentality in those who claim, "All I know is the streets." All the while, such individuals do not consider that the world is so much bigger than the streets. So again, I say, do not relegate your reality to the streets. This is like complaining about how horrible your conditions are but yet spending your whole life refusing to go anywhere else. The idea of the streets is something we choose to believe in, so it is also something we can choose not to believe in. And by not embracing this idea, you will less likely become a victim to it.

Because of how engrained this idea is in our culture, you have to make it your objective to not become a statistic of the streets, thus, you should aim to shamelessly dissociate your identity from the streets. Do not allow the culture to pressure you into adopting this idea as if by not doing so would make you a lesser version of yourself. If you plan to have children, also be careful about conveying a sense of pride in this idea because children will naturally adopt the ideas of their parents. Instead, condition your children to see the idea of the streets as the illusion it truly is. Condition to them to see it as something lame and ignorant. Make no mistake, I am not telling you to hate and despise all those who subscribe to such an idea, because to do so would serve you no purpose. Rather, I am telling you to be self-aware of the perils of this idea so that you yourself never fall victim to it. I just want you to understand its limitations and eventualities. Make yourself accustomed to recognizing those who operate by such ideas so that you can avoid being influenced and if you have already identified with such an idea, you must deconstruct it from your consciousness.

Don't champion the streets as if it's some honor you embrace for yourself. Don't take pride in the fact that your father was in the streets because this was also what brought about his downfall. Be someone that looks through the surface of the streets having seen what it has done to you and your people. Understand that it has brought about the fragmentation of your family. Realize that it has contributed to the death, incarceration, and stagnation of many of the men and women of your own family. If you can manage to escape the pressures of identifying yourself with the streets, you will have avoided a generational obstacle that would have surely swallowed you as it has all those before you; by overcoming this obstacle you will have broaden your perspective as well as augmented your potential. Be someone who breaks the cycle for not just yourself but for those who will come behind you. Since your father has failed to do so, my hope is that you will be successful.

Love Dad

Section 3

Personal Development

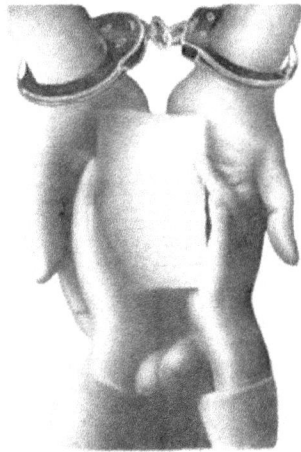

18

The Jewel of Purity

Dear Daughter

There has never been a time in human history when jewelry was not treasured. Our obsession with jewelry is demonstrated by how we value it based on its degree of purity. Thus, jewelry is the few things in life people will always and forever desire in its purest form. Similarly, women are also regarded as one of life's treasures. And like jewelry, the degree of true value we attribute to a woman will always correlate with her degree of purity. Even biblical scripture acknowledges that there are very few things in life as valuable as a pure woman.

And while there are many things capable of tainting a woman's purity, nothing is more susceptible to such than the instrument from which she brings about life. God has made woman the rightful overseer of the function of life. Therefore, your purity as a woman will first and foremost be assessed by how you oversee this function. So more than anything else, it is your modesty, which stands to purify or de-purify your essence as a woman.

For this reason, the way in which you perceive the idea of sex is of the upmost importance. My hope is that you come to approach this *idea of sex as something sacred. For how could an act that brings about something as transcendent as life be anything but sacred. But your task of approaching sex with a virtuous perception is no doubt a difficult one as we live in a society that aims to desecrate the sanctity of this idea. This explains why sex is so supercharged and commercialized. Everywhere you look, you will see sex being sensationalized, having now been relegated from something intimate and hallow to something explicit and sacrilegious. My daughter do not allow yourself to conceive of the idea of sex in the way society will have you conceive it. Because if not careful, it will cause you to lose your purity in a way that you can never again retain it. The key is to approach this idea with the right mindset. And the right mindset is not allowing yourself to become infatuated with the experience of sex itself. While the experience of sex is a beautiful fruit of life, like anything else, an obsession with it can lead to disastrous consequences.*

Unfortunately, you will have sexual desire. As much as I would love for this not to be the case, it is inevitable. Thus, you will certainly struggle with the same urges and passions that all human beings experience. But for the most part, these sexual impulses will more often be collateral to your experience. Which means, these impulses will oftentimes be stimulated from what you see, hear, and feel in your environment. This includes the TV shows you watch, the music you listen to and the immoral disposition of society itself. The frequency in which you experience such impulses will oftentimes be a direct result of your exposure to this sex crazed culture; a culture aiming to provide you a liberal mentality of the idea of sex. For young women, there is immense pressure to cave in to this idea that sex has no bearing on one's virtue but being a woman of integrity; your struggle should be one of resistance to such an idea. Do not succumb to your every sexual desire like so many other girls will do. Do not give in to your any and every whim. Do not just claim to have morals and principles but employ them by being someone who exercises physical self-control and discipline. Assert the willpower God has given you by practicing self-restraint. For the flames of desire will only burn sporadically, they do not last. So be strong-minded and let them burn out when they arise rather than extinguishing them with self-indulgence. Because the fires you prematurely extinguish through indulgent gratification will more quickly reignite than those you allow to burn out naturally.

We live in such a sick world, one where you are sure to be considered weird or different if you do not succumb to the pressure of sexuality. Nowadays if you do not demonstrate an insatiable sexual appetite, you will undoubtedly have your womanhood questioned and it may sadly be by the same women that should be encouraging you to preserve your modesty. This culture we occupy is backwards. As you go about the business of preserving your purity, and maintaining your integrity, consider those who hinder your pursuit nothing short of ignorant. You will see many women taking pride in some of the most insignificant things in life, but let your pride be in the respect you have for yourself.

The key to mastering your sexual urges is in mastering your self-restraint. Many individuals have succumbed to their passions to the extent that they are actually being controlled by their sexual desire with even realizing it. These people are like slaves. The woman who cannot stop having children is most likely a slave to her own sexual urges. These are weak-minded individuals. Do not become such a woman, as it is unbecoming of who you are to be such, for you my daughter are royalty. You were born to rule and control, not to be ruled and controlled over. And you will never be capable of controlling anything of substance until you are first capable of controlling yourself. As you go about the business of mastering yourself, make it a regular habit to fast as the Muslims fast. Nothing will help you master yourself more than the practice of abstaining from bodily nourishment. As there is no appetite more potent than the one, we have for food and drink. If you are able to subdue these appetites and urges through fasting, you will more readily subdue any sexual urges that may come.

Love Dad

19

Jewel of Mental Health

Dear Daughter,

How are you my beautiful Daughter? As always, my focus remains centered on the very truth I stand on, from which I hold dearly to my grasp of Reality. In a world where everyone seems to be becoming more and more delusional and out of touch with truth, it can become difficult not to lose one's sanity. Which is exactly why mental health is considered the most prevalent disorder in society with no curative measure in sight. And how could there ever be a curative measure when there is no grasp of what mental health is truly about.

Above any and everything else, a mental health condition is both a spiritual and psychological state of losing touch with one's reality. For this reason, your grasp of reality must now become as important to you as the air you breathe. Nowadays reality is something we cannot do without; therefore, you must find it, cling to it, and never let it go. But there is only one way in which this can be done and it is through your inner heart. People tend to lose touch with reality by their inability to get out of their own head or by immersing themselves too deeply in their own thoughts. This has led to the rise of meditational practices such as yoga and other disciplines aimed at quieting the mind. But those who waste time with such practices do not realize that the true problem lies in their misidentifying the self. Think briefly for a second, from where exactly is your true self emanating? Most people are convinced that their awareness protrudes from the brain. Thus, they experience life through the prism of their thoughts. We fail to realize that we are not our thoughts. The reason we have this psychological struggle to get out of our own head is because we have yet to pinpoint where the true self resides, which is within the heart. The mis- orientation of the self is what is truly causing people to lose touch with reality. So again, the only way to maintain one's grasp of reality is by correctly identifying the locality of one's true self. Thus, the practice of tending to your internal inner heart will always anchor you to Reality.

Many people will also lose touch with reality as a result of the type of ideas they internalize. You must always remain aware of what ideas you allow into your heart. Because once the heart internalizes an idea, it then becomes a part of you. You will hear stories about people who seemed normal and stable who then all of sudden, did something completely insane. It will be said that these people went crazy, but the truth is whatever insane act that individual committed was merely a product of the insane idea they internalized. Remember, our ideas will always come back to haunt us, sometimes in the most unpredictable of ways.

It may even be the case that we invest so much of our belief in a certain idea, that it becomes a subjective reality in itself. For this reason, if ever you run into someone hopelessly delusional about some matter; do not bother wasting your time trying to help. Such individuals are those who come to believe in an idea so strongly that it eventually becomes their subjective reality. Oftentimes, these individuals will opt to remain in these realities rather than in true reality. For example, you might run into the woman who refuses to see the truth about her significant other, even when it is apparent to everyone else. Such women refuse to accept any reality other than one where she and her significant other are together. If you pay attention, you will notice many people in such conditions to many different things. And the longer these people occupy these subjective realities, the more out of touch with true reality they become.

My daughter, be certain you are operating in truth and in reality, rather than some in subjective reality. Stay thoroughly in tune with Reality, as there are those in this world who are deceivers by nature. Never take into your intimacy anyone entrenched in their delusions. Because developing a bond with such individuals can only be done by entertaining their delusions, which will eventually have you questioning your reality and ultimately your sanity. Once you have a firm grip of reality, make it a point not to allow liars and deceivers into your intimacy. Because liars, deceivers, and illusional situations are the very things that will rob you of your sanity, or more accurately your Reality. Therefore, again, I tell you that one of the most important things in life is reality. Strive to find true Reality as it is rather than reality as you presume it to be. By doing this, you ensure yourself to never be undone by any mental health condition.

Love Dad

20

Jewel of Wise Decisions

Dear Daughter,

How are you? There are times that I look around and think to myself, how in the world did I end up here? In these moments, I have to remind myself that it was nothing more than my choices that have piloted my path thus far. As you begin your journey just know that your choices will ultimately serve as the navigation system of your life. And this doesn't just apply to the major life choices you make, this also includes the choices you think may be insignificant. Absolutely everything is contingent on the choices we make. As every single choice serves as doors we open to particular paths in life; therefore, you must use your third eye to perceive which doors are conducive to your success and which are detrimental to your wellbeing. Because in most cases, once you make a choice, and proceed through a particular door, there is no turning back. And wherever it is that door takes you will be where you have to go whether willingly or unwillingly.

Therefore, you must strive to make yourself an exceptional choice-maker on a consistent basis. And becoming such an individual requires you to develop profound insight; something generally *acquired through a relative understanding of history. As many others have previously made all of the same choices that lie before you, it is in their experience that you will find further understanding of what a choice entails and whether or not it is worth your choosing. For this reason, you must strive to become a student of history. Begin by first familiarizing yourself with the history of those you share a common lineage with; this includes anything you can learn from or about the lives of your parents, grandparents, and great grandparents as their history will provide you a reflection of your history. Afterwards you should then familiarize yourself with the histories of those you both admire and despise. As this will show you exactly which choices are most conducive to becoming the woman you wish to be as well as those that will lead to you becoming someone you do not wish to be.*

When you piece together every single choice we make in life, they will collectively outline our complete story. Let this show you the gravity of your choices. There are certain things that occur outside of our control, but seldom will such things serve as determining factors of the course of our affairs. In most cases, it is our decisions that will dictate our outcome. Now make no mistake, this does not mean the outcome of your choices will always coincide with your desires, hopes and dreams, but rather the outcome of your choices will always be a product of your guiding influence. We create our lives by nothing more but the choices we make. It is almost a paradox how the tiniest life choices can cause the greatest impacts. The same decision that may seem trivial and inconsequential today may eventually come to underlie the overall state of your affairs tomorrow. Make sure to be aware, alert, and conscientious of every single choice you make. Because in the end, that will be the determining factor of not just some things but everything.

Love Dad

21

Jewel of Understanding Pleasures

Dear Daughter,

I pray this letter reach you in the best of states. States that are only conducive to your growth and progress intellectually, emotionally, and spiritually. The life we have in this world is much too short; it passes us by ever so quickly. But this demonstrates the nature of our purpose here in this world. This temporary life correlates with the temporary task we are destined to accomplish. Finding this God given task is predicated on our willingness to seek; searching to find the very thing God put us here to discover. As your father, I would love to save you from the trouble of searching and tell you what your task is but this is something no parent can do for a child. I have not a clue as to what your God given task is in life. This is the one of the few things in life everyone must come to realize for themselves. Nonetheless, what I can assure you is that you were certainly not put here to solely seek out is pleasure. And this is not merely my opinion, but a biological truth.

Even in our most heated passions and deepest desires, we are subject to an appetitive capacity; and once those appetites become satisfied our very anatomies disincline us to indulge any further. For example, there are certain foods that bring us immense pleasure, but if you eat enough of that food there will come a point that your stomach will ache, and it will become almost impossible to further digest anything else regardless of how pleasurable the food. Hobbies such as reading or exercising one's intellectual capacities can bring us immense pleasure but after an extended period, there comes a point when our anatomies will physically prevent us from continuing any further. We get dizzy, restless, our eyes get heavy, our hands, neck, or back begin to cramp and we are then forced to take a break. And lastly what desire is there more intense than the act of sex. But even sex has its physical limitations. Because at a certain point, our sexual organs will not allow us to continue the act regardless of how pleasurable the experience.

How could it be that God would create us solely for the sake of pleasure but provide us with physical anatomies specifically designed to limit such? It would also seem nonsensical to create a world for the purpose of pleasure but then allow there to be so much pain, tragedy, and misfortune. How irrational would it be for God to give us lives to exclusively seek out pleasures, but then create us to die so swiftly? But far be it from God to be either nonsensical or irrational. Therefore, we can conclude that we were not put here solely for the pursuit of pleasures. Thus, my love, you must not become a pleasure-seeker. There are women whose entire existence is predicated on the indulgence of pleasure. They eat not to sustain themselves but to pleasure themselves. All of their ideas, beliefs, and perspectives are all byproducts of their pleasures.

And their biggest accomplishments in life will only be experiences that offered them the opportunity to gratify their deepest pleasures. These types of women typically have no self-- control, self-respect and are prone to self-sabotage. In unconscious pursuit of their pleasures, there is no line they won't cross, loyalty they won't betray, nor trust they won't break. And as a result, they will eventually ruin all of their opportunities, relationships, friendships, and kinships. Daughter, is this the type of woman you really want to be? One whose whole existence is predicated on pleasure.

Not only should you not become this type of woman, you should also not surround yourself with such women.

We should never allow ourselves to be consumed by any pleasure. For life will naturally bring us our fair share of pleasures without us obsessively having to seek them. As a woman of dignity, if you are to consume yourself with anything, let it be with what provides you the most self-fulfillment. Or let it be with what provides you the most enlightenment. Do not limit your pleasures only to the carnal flesh. Let your pleasures derive also from your intellect, from your spirit. Let your pleasure be in doing what inspires you. Let your pleasure be in what makes you feel the most alive. Let it be in what makes you feel important. Let it be participating in something transcendent and life changing. Let it be in breaking down barriers, interrupting the status quo and shattering the mold. Let it be accomplishing what no one else believed you could accomplish, doing what know no one believed you could do and being who no one else believed you could be. Let your pleasure be in finding something no one else could find or going somewhere no one else would go. These are the pleasures you should more readily tend to, as these are the pleasures that do not lower one's integrity but elevates it. All in all, strive not be a pleasure-seeker as such individuals ultimately become slaves to their pleasures. When you encounter the individual who is obese, a drug addict, or a nympho understand that these are in most cases the individuals who allowed themselves to become pleasure seekers. Train yourself to be content without pleasure. For example, if you have a choice between the plate of chocolate cake and the plate of green grapes, train yourself to incline to the healthier choice, which is in most cases the choice of least pleasure. It is rare to find such individuals with the will to choose progress over pleasure but in the same breath, it is even rarer to find someone successful with a heart given to pleasure seeking. Those preoccupied with pleasure are rarely successful at anything.

Love Dad

22

The Jewel of Acceptance

Dear Daughter

I pray this letter reaches you in a state of contentment and fulfillment and that your sense of purpose helps you to accept the things you cannot change, because the worst state one can occupy is that of discontentment. The world is so full of people looking to enhance any and every characteristic of themselves due to their deep- seated discontent. This is why every year billions of dollars are spent on plastic surgery, sexual enhancements, beauty products, and health and fitness supplements. The mass consumption of such products reflects the prevailing dissatisfaction in society. People are discontent with everything, whether it be their parents, friends, hair, skin complexion, just about everything!

As a society, we celebrate certain individuals for being ambitious and successful when in reality, the impetus driving such individuals is all too often an overwhelming discontent with what they cannot accept; or in other words, an inability to accept their reality. When someone refuses to accept their reality, it puts them in a state of denial. With the tendency we have to attach ourselves to certain ideas, we are all subject to being in denial about something that is blatantly clear to everyone else, which can oftentimes lead to our downfall. Anything we dislike, we refuse to accept. We embark upon life so discontented with everything about ourselves we reject anything but what we believe to be true. This is perhaps why the show American Idol is so fascinating to me. Because it exposes just how many people live in a state of denial about something they cannot accept. Many musicians refuse to accept that they are not gifted singers because in their obsessive pursuit to force reality to conform to what they want it to be, they become delusional, maniacal, or even deranged to some extent. The refusal to accept what we cannot change imprisons us in stagnation. When you are unable to accept what has no reality in your life, you are blinded to what unexpected things life does give reality to. Just imagine devoting your entire life to becoming a singer, never to realize how good you are at math. Here you are trying to be the next Miley Cyrus when you could be the second coming to Albert Einstein. This is the reality of those who refuse to accept their reality.

My deepest hope is that you not be one of these individuals; that you not allow the culture, your family, or your desires to ever render you dissatisfied with what you were apportioned in life. My daughter do not relegate your life to just a search for overcompensation because to do so deprives you of the meaningfulness of life. There is a world of people who have wasted valuable time and relationships because of their inability to accept what they could not change. These individuals squander their true potential by self-absorbing themselves with their dissatisfaction rather than focusing on maximizing their potential.

Your acceptance of the things you cannot change is both the door to your emotional freedom and the key to unlocking your deepest potential. We must always maintain the capacity to accept our reality no matter what the circumstances because acceptance is the first prerequisite to identifying and removing one's self-delusion. And in essence, the removal of one's self-delusion is the beginning of self-mastery. You will hear people talk of loving oneself and being true to oneself but it is impossible to do such without first reaching a degree of acceptance with oneself. The realization of this state of acceptance is the most liberating and empowering state one can ever attain. Acceptance is the true source of charisma, aura, and appeal, all of which are requisites to be a great leader.

I urge you to exercise your personal acceptance as soon as possible. Do not waste the best years of your life fearing how others may react. It always requires more energy to fear something than it does to let go and not care. Many people will allow life to overwhelm them to the extent that they reach their acceptance after having allowed their adversity to get the best of them. In such situations, acceptance does not benefit the individual because of the bitterness that permeates one's heart as a result. When you are finally able to accept what you cannot change, you remove the burden weighing you down thus allowing you to maneuver in a way that inspires others to embrace their acceptance. My daughter, what you will come to realize is that one of the most debilitating fears people have is the truth. Most people cringe at the idea of having to face the truth. But the one who has already accepted their reality and their truth will not be threatened or unsettled by anything. Because what can be left to fear after having accepted the reality of what you fear the most? This naturally provides you all the courage you could ever need.

The sooner you reach acceptance, the sooner your true journey will begin. People spend so much of their lives climbing their through self-deception, fear and naivety that by the time they reach a state of acceptance, they have no energy left to partake of the real journey. Acceptance is not tantamount to defeat; acceptance is the ability to fight uninhibitedly. Acceptance allows you to withdraw all the precious energy you have been wasting on useless and unattainable pursuits and redirect them to endeavors conducive to your betterment. There are a lot of people in dire need of change, people who want nothing more but to change and to start over. But in most cases, these individuals will never aspire to true change because of their inability to accept their current reality. If only they knew that acceptance is the prerequisite for change. My daughter, I love you and my hope is that you reach your personal acceptance.

Love Dad

23

Jewel of Wealth

Dear Daughter,

I pray this letter enables you understand the value of stability, security, and economic freedom. Because as a woman, there will be very few things more important for you than financial security. This is not to say that money is the most important thing in life but that the lack thereof makes life so much more complicated, especially for women. Here we are in the year 2024 and we still live in a society that still pays men an average salary higher than that of women who do the same job. Therefore, you must resolve to be someone who has financial security. But in order to have financial security, you must first understand the essence of finance or in other words, the essence of money. The idea of money is best understood in relation to the idea of an economy. If our economy were an electrical circuit, money would serve as the electrical voltage providing an input as well as an output. When you understand the concept of an economy and the way money functions within it, you realize it is essentially comprised of three parts: regulators, consumers, and producers. The regulators are the financial entities and institutions such as the

U.S. Treasury, Banks, and Wall Street that all serve to balance and stabilize the economy. Regulators serve as the power source of the economy. Next, are the producers, which are the distributors, entrepreneurs, business owners, and merchandisers, which all serve to stimulate and disseminate the flow of money and goods throughout the economy. Producers are the means of input within the circuit. And lastly and most importantly are the consumers, which are those who work to produce money and goods for the sole purpose of consuming them. Thus, the consumers are the means of the output for this circuit. But the consumers are perhaps the most important component of the economy because these individuals contribute to all three tasks by aiding in the regulation, production, and consumption thereby perfecting this cycle of continuous input and output. The viability of any economic circuit depends on consumers who ironically derive the least value from this system.

In essence, what I am telling you is that the reason poor people remain poor is that they will always use what little money they have to consume, rather than produce. The majority of people around you will be takers, taking what they can get just to give it back to the economy. Those we consider wealthy are not wealthy because they merely possess money; they are wealthy by virtue of their ability to generate money and not just for themselves but rather for the economy. When one becomes a generator of vast amounts of money for the economy, it inadvertently provides you with more influence over the direction of the economy. When you are a direct producer of energy for the economy, you become almost an overseer. Therefore, being rich is more so a product of the degree of influence one exercises over the flow of money rather than the amount one owns. Money is an active phenomenon not meant to be possessed. Much like electricity, it must always be in movement; otherwise, it loses its potency. As I told you earlier, money and economy are interconnected ideas. You cannot understand one without understanding the other. For you personally my daughter, what this means is you must find your means to produce in whatever capacity that may be; if in fact it is your objective not to live paycheck to paycheck for the rest of your life. You must refrain yourself from becoming the impulsive and overindulgent consumers. Strive to learn economics, because in understanding the larger economy you will have provided yourself a basis to better manage your financial condition. Thus, allowing you to operate your personal economy with precision. By learning the nature of money, you understand its language, habits, and motions and this will allow you mastery in budgeting your cash flow, investing, saving, and spending.

As mentioned earlier, those we consider rich, or wealthy are not considered so merely because of the money they possess. Instead, such individuals are considered wealthy because of the assets they own. Assets not only provide the owner a means to more monetary value but they are also the only tangible form of value that exists. While money on the other hand, is only a symbol of value. If our current financial institution were to nose-dive, paper money could lose all worth, while assets would retain much of their value. Thus, when one owns an asset, they will always be wealthier than one who merely possesses a lot of paper money. Wealth has never been predicated on money alone, but rather on stake, controlling interest, equity, and ownership. Never consider someone rich simply because they have money, instead consider what assets they own and how much energy those assets are inputting into the economy. This will tell you the true value of one's wealth. My point is simply to demonstrate that your first true goal as an overseer of your personal economy should be to secure your own assets, specifically your own home. As a woman, there is nothing more fulfilling than knowing you own something. Furthermore, this asset would provide you with the equity necessary to acquire money that can be used to further invest in additional assets or new businesses that would further help to stimulate your economy. This is how you become a producer. Furthermore, if you were to oversee your economy with precision and astuteness, you could perhaps then transform your asset or business into a financial institution that could potentially stabilize the greater economy. This would then make you a regulator! Such a feat would put you in the top one percent of people in this world that controls the global economy. Not even Oprah or Beyonce have reached this level. In essence, this is the path to building true wealth.

But building wealth and earning money is not always a matter of doing something you're most passionate about. Because it might be the case that what you are passionate about is not what the majority of consumers are passionate about. Producers are those who produce what the greater population is most passionate about, while they themselves may not be the least bit moved by it. Therefore, remember, regardless of the service, good, or product you produce, you must ensure that it is something essential to the needs or desires of the greater population.

Love Dad

Additional Books by Marcus Swan

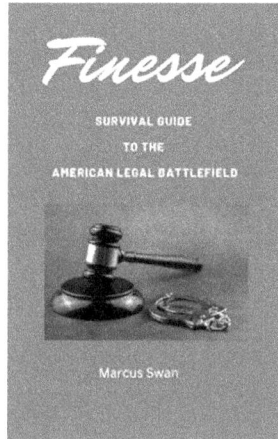

www.ingramcontent.com/pod-product-compliance
Lightning Source LLC
Chambersburg PA
CBHW072148090426
42741CB00026B/1262